AF540412

THE FATHER OF INDIAN CIVIL AVIATION
J.R.D. TATA
A COMPLETE BIOGRAPHY

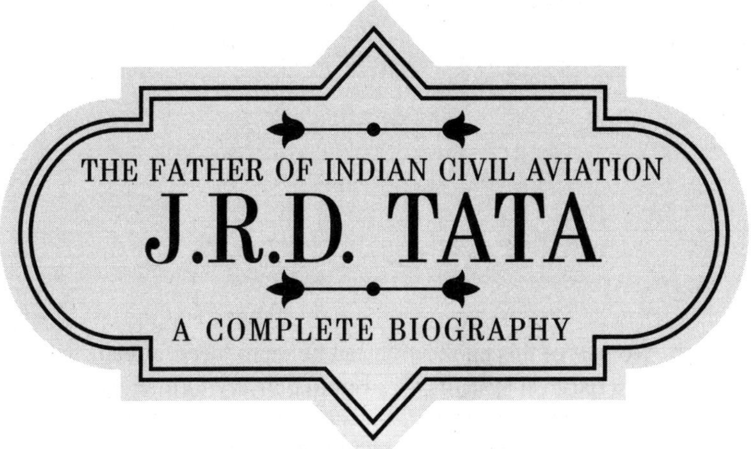

VINOD SHARMA

Published by
PRABHAT PRAKASHAN PVT. LTD.
4/19 Asaf Ali Road,
New Delhi-110 002 (INDIA)
e-mail: prabhatbooks@gmail.com

ISBN 978-93-5562-070-5
J.R.D. TATA : A COMPLETE BIOGRAPHY
by Shri Vinod Sharma

Edition
2026

Paperback Price
₹ 300.00 (Rupees Three Hundred only)

Printed at
R-Tech Offset Printers, Delhi

Author's Note

In the pages that follow, we delve into the extraordinary life of one of India's most iconic industrialists and father of Indian civil aviation - Jehangir Ratanji Dadabhoy Tata, fondly known as J.R.D. Tata. Born in Paris in 1904, J.R.D. Tata became an iconic entrepreneur and aviation trailblazer, leaving an indelible mark on India's industrial evolution.

From his early years, J.R.D. displayed a remarkable blend of vision and determination. His involvement in the Tata Group, a conglomerate founded by his family, soon led him to the helm of the company. Through his visionary leadership, J.R.D. transformed the Tata Group from a traditional business into a global powerhouse, fostering industries ranging from steel to aviation.

Educated across continents, including France, Japan, and England, J.R.D. Tata's path initially led him to the French army. Yet, the call of his family's legacy beckoned, and he returned to India in 1925, assuming a pivotal role in the Tata family business.

As the pioneer of civil aviation in India, J.R.D. Tata founded Air India, connecting the nation to the world's skies. His unrelenting pursuit of excellence was mirrored not only in business but also in his commitment to social welfare, leading to the establishment of philanthropic institutions that continue to impact lives. That very year marked the commencement of the first scheduled service, dedicated to flying mail on select routes for what was then known as Imperial Airways.

Throughout his life, J.R.D. Tata championed innovation, ethics, and community development. His contributions, such as the Tata Institute of Social Sciences and Tata Memorial Hospital, stand as a testament to his dedication to societal progress.

In chronicling the life of J.R.D. Tata, I hope to capture not only his business acumen but also his unwavering commitment to India's growth. Through this narrative, I aspire to bring to light lesser-known facets of his life, providing readers from all walks of life an opportunity to be inspired by his remarkable story.

May this biography serve as a reminder that the pursuit of excellence, compassion, and dedication can shape not only individual destinies but also the destiny of a nation.

Contents

❑

The History of the History

Esplanade House, Bombay.
23rd Nov. 1898

Dear Swami Vivekananda,

I trust, you remember me as a fellow-traveller on your voyage from Japan to Chicago. I very much recall at this moment your views on the growth of the ascetic spirit in India, and the duty, not of destroying, but of diverting it into useful channels.

I recall these ideas in connection with my scheme of Research Institute of Science for India, of which you have doubtless heard or read. It seems to me that no better use can be made of the ascetic spirit than the establishment of monasteries or residential halls for men dominated by this spirit, where they should live with ordinary decency and devote their lives to the cultivation of sciences—natural and humanistic.

I am of opinion that if such a crusade in favour of an asceticism of this kind were undertaken by a competent leader, it would greatly help asceticism, science, and the good name of our common country; and I know not who would make a more fitting general of such a campaign than Vivekananda.

Do you think you would care to apply yourself to the mission of galvanising into life our ancient traditions in this respect? Perhaps, you had better begin with a fiery pamphlet rousing our people in this matter. I would cheerfully defray all the expenses of publication.

With kind regards,
I am, dear Swami,
Yours faithfully,
JAMSETJI TATA

The year was 1893. The scorching heat of May summer was devouring the eastern endurance of luxury and commitment, Nature was suffocated and the people of Bengal were feeling a sense of illusion, the vultures in the rural front were planning to record the anecdotes of the human sacrifice, and the entire motion was gluttonised by the antipathy of sentiment. At this very moment of painted melancholy, small bubbles of a surmounting history were getting elevated slowly, silently as well as utter steadily. (Author please simplify first para) On 31 May of the same year, a steamer sailing to Vancouver from Yokohama surprisingly became a tacit witness of a captivating encounter between the two august souls of India – the sender of the above letter and obviously the receiver at the far end.

Jamsetji was planning to sail for an industrial exposition in Chicago. (Author: what is industrial renunciation) He was a very frequent visitor to Japan, and was staying at the same hotel where Swami Vivekananda was about to register in the next few days. The duo began their journey from Yokohama to the Canadian port of Vancouver aboard the SS Empress of India, a 16,992 ton luxury queen of ocean, owned by Canadian Pacific Steamship Company.

Though the duo had met earlier, but Jamsetji and Vivekananda never got sufficient time to be engaged in a full-fledged conversation. The opportunity then arrived. Swamiji recounted the experiences he had gained during his visits throughout India as a wandering monk to quench his thirst for truth and wisdom. He narrated about the relentless domination of millions of Indians, ordinary and subaltern people, at the hands of the colonisers. He also informed

Jamsetji about the treasures of Sanskrit and Bengali manuscripts he had found in different Buddhist monasteries during his visit to China. Swamiji explained that to carry his faith to the West and praying for unity among world's top religions was the mission of his visit to the World Parliament of Religions in Chicago.

They also discussed about Japan's phenomenal progress in the field of technology as they had observed. Jamsetji now disclosed to Vivekananda his mission, and that was to establish India's own steel industry. He also explained that he had been in search of proper equipment and technological support that could make India a wealthy nation in terms of industrial development. And if one heavy industry got introduced, there must be some ancillary industries to base the backbone of the supreme. Thus India would get strengthened in technological fluidity. (Author check Fluidity) Vivekananda endorsed Jamsetji's vision with enthusiasm and added that instead of importing matches from Japan, Jamsetji should manufacture those in India to secure the livelihood of the rural poor. The founder of one of India's largest conglomerates and the spiritual maestro understood that the real hope of India lay in the prosperity and development of its groundlings. The industry would save their fortune and would reduce the havoc of financial crisis which the ordinary millions generally succumbed to.

The conversation between these two great personalities was unknowingly inseminating the seeds of future establishment of one of the world's most significant and powerful industries, not only to serve humanity, but also to be reciprocated by the cultural and immensely potential artifacts long hidden in the inset of ordinary millions. (Author check line meaning potential artifacts?)The crisis of identity in the labourers was one of the toughest problems at that time. India, as being the advertent storehouse of the eternal existence of religious conundrum, (Author pls check para) remains in favour of a psychologically paradigmatic worldview of limited stereotypes and the industrialisation lasts in a handful of masters who deplete every drop of their blood and sweat to ensure perpetuation of their proud lineage. Jamsetji, the born-Parsee Gujarati magician, built the nation's pride—Tata Group of Companies, and a city was founded with his name —Jamshedpur.

❑

An Era of Fulfilment

Jamsetji Nusserwanjee Tata was the first visionary industrialist to initiate industrial development in India in the era of industrial revolution, following the idea of Swamiji, manufacturing the materials solely on the basis of 'desi' machineries. It is he, who for the first time in India established the steel plant, the first hydro-electric project and a university of science, over which the colonisers could feel jealous of, as they did not have that much simultaneously in parallel. This university had different departments for post-graduate courses, specially, in electrical, mechanical and civil engineering, and also in various aspects of humanities. It would enable students also to research into India's national history, to study Indian archaeology and other Indian affairs.

Jamsetji created his wealth through textiles. In the late nineteenth century, when capitalism all over the world was at its peak, he initiated a pension scheme for his workers and also planned an insurance policy for his mill workers that would help their family with a secured livelihood, and accident compensation if a bolt from the blue should take place. Jamsetji was miles ahead of his fellow competitors and decades ahead of his time.

Though the tinctures of capitalist outlook (Author ch phrase, meaning of tinctures of capitalist outlook) might not be ignored, it was evident that the super-monopoly of a furnished empire gets immediately drained up by the lethargy and the nonchalant approach from the coming-up ancestors and every historical kingdom had suffered this same issue of tumbling "headlong down" after some years of its overwhelming climax. Be it of Guptas after Skandagupta or of Mughals after Aurangzeb in India, or of seminal Byzantine civilisation after Justinian, every delicacy of an empire (Author ch phrase) ends up with the arrival of an Icarus following a successful Daedalus, and the resistance towards the exterior propagandas gets shattered, the fundamental base gets demolished. But, here comes the group of Tata, where, till now, the benchmark remains unsatisfied, and so generation after generation is searching the way to its peak, continuously mounting higher, in spite of the exotic animosity (author : exotic animosity meaning) and other fellow reasons.(Author check simplify para)

Jamsetji had the entire plan set for their erection but disaster came in his life in the form of untimely death on 19 May 1904. At that time, neither the steel plant nor the hydro-electric power supply company had been floated, nor had the University of Science been started. In the next few years, Dorab, the son of legendary Jamsetji Tata and Ratanji Dadabhoy Tata, the cousin of the same iconic figure, teamed up together to make Jamsetji's dream come true. Though earlier they had a strained relationship, but after Jamsetji's death, they collaborated to realise his dream. Their teaming up is again suggestive of the fact that is, the close bonding of the Tatas and development, for which individualism could be sacrificed but the grand service could not wait further.

The man of steel was buried honourably in Brookwood cemetery in England at the end of May, 1904. The void after his passing away was soon eased as just after seventy days of Jamsetji's death, Ratanji Dadabhoy Tata's second child, a son, was born in Paris on 29 July. They gave him a Persian name—"Jehangir", meaning the "conqueror of the world". The namereminds us of the Mughal emperor, and this child,

Jehangir, would very soon be on the path of becoming the 'Tata Tycoon', and take after the emperor in his own way—of perpetual grandeur in terms of proliferation of industries and service to humanity.

❑

The Season of Legacy

Paris, the connoisseur city of art and culture for a long long time, is hugely responsible for the flourish of cultural elevation in the West. One can recall the development of 'colonised' England after the advent of other communities one by one, and one of the most significant impacts was after the inevitable Norman Conquest of 1066 AD. William of Normandy defeated England in the Battle of Hastings and the governance of England fell into the hands of the French. After this super-edification, (Author check word super-edification) England flourished astonishingly due to the

French influence on different milieus, right from language to culture, art to knowledge of everything. Various theatre halls, art gallerys, statues and other grand buildings were established that showcased the vivacious French glory. At the heart of the cultural life of Paris, then as now, stands L'Opera or The Palais Garnier. It has been called "probably the most famous opera house in the world, a symbol of Paris like Notre Dame Cathedral, the Louvre, or the Sacré Coeur Basilica." But here the importance of one of the 9th arrondissements of France is only to highlight the lane beside a spacious road named Rue de Halevy. The second house on Rue de Halevy is fairly modern and it must have been almost new when R.D. Tata's family occupied it in 1904. It was there that JRD was born. It has a magnificent entrance, its curved doors almost as high as Westminster Abbey's, probably to provide a hint to the newborn's towering stature in his later life.

Jehangir, later to be called Jeh, recalls his early years (vide: Lala, R. M. (1992). *Beyond the Last Blue Mountain: The Authorised Biography of JRD Tata.)*:

'My childhood and youth, so different from those of the average middle class Parsee, were mainly conditioned by the fact that my father had married a Frenchwoman, and we spent half of our early years in Paris and half in Bombay. My father loved life in France, French food and wines, and because my mother was at first not familiar with the English language, the language used by all of us was French. What I remember most vividly is that we always seemed to be on the move, and that my lovely and cultured mother had to uproot herself every two years or so to find a new home—alternately in France and in India. With servants and office help available in India, her task whenever we arrived in India or left was relatively simple. But in France, where our domestic help consisted of never more than a maid and a cook, the job of finding a new apartment, furnishing it while looking after her growing brood—there were five of us—represented a real chore which she accomplished with amazing efficiency and apparent ease but at the cost of much fatiguing work.'

One of the various problems Jehangir faced early on was that of language, because of his mixed heritage: 'When I attended one of the government schools in Paris, the Anson De Sally, I was a much better student in French than I was in English at the Cathedral School in Bombay.' (*Beyond the Last Blue Mountain,* R.M. Lala)

Anyway, though the language barrier was considerable, Cathedral School in Bombay bored him a lot. He found no reason why he should learn British official history, the recorded history of the colonisers. He recalls: 'I used to ask "But what happened in India?" I have a good recollection of asking: "What about Aurangzeb?" and being smacked down. I don't know why I chose Aurangzeb!' (*Beyond the Last Blue Mountain,* R.M. Lala)

He had immense interest in Mathematics and Physics. He shared more about his school-memories: 'My first important memories from the point of view of a growing child, blessed with a fairly observant and inquisitive mind, were about cars and aeroplanes. My father decided that we needed a home of our own in which to spend our holidays, and he picked on a new and developing beach resort on the Channel coast of France, south of Boulogne, called Hardelot, where he not only bought a villa but later on built a number of villas and shops as a real estate developer. In fact, one of the two main streets of Hardelot was officially named Avenue des Indes.

'It happened that the legendary Louis Bleriot, who acquired world fame in1909 by being the first to fly a plane across the Channel, also chose Hardelot for his family's summer resort. Bleriot built not only a fine villa close to ours but also a hangar nearing the beach. On the beach his personal plane used to land much to the excitement of everyone there—grown-ups and children, none more starry-eyed than myself. From then on I was hopelessly hooked on aeroplanes and made up my mind that, come what may, one day I would be a pilot. I had to wait many years for that dream to come true.' (*Beyond the Last Blue Mountain,* R.M. Lala)

France was a prosperous country, with a vibrant culture, exceptional literature and all of its cities (mostly Paris) filled with people nurturing aesthetic, artistic qualities. In each and every town and village of France there were philosophers with profound knowledge and innovative ideologies, teenagers with avid reading habits along with a love for paintings, sculptures, frescos and so on. There existed groups and societies who were fond of cultural performances and they would go to the theatre halls every week to replenish their stock of ideas and enrich their minds. Not only as a viewer, they would review the performances and send it to different entertainment magazines of contemporary times while others would subscribe to them. It was that golden time when Jehangir was slowly growing up in such a socially progressive environment.When the First World War began in 1914, Jehangir's father R.D. was in Bombay, (now Mumbai). Jehangir was spending a holiday in Switzerland with his granny, and Sooni, Jehangir's beloved mother remained in Paris. She started to work at the American Hospital in Paris and devoted her time in the service of ordinary men and soldiers. Jehangir clearly remembers, when her mother came at the station to receive him and his siblings after their holiday, they were shocked to see her in the white apron of a nurse.

In Paris, Jehangir was getting accustomed to the air raids on his city. The first time the raid happened, Jehangir was on the terrace. In his words: 'We were in the shadow of the Eiffel Tower and from the terrace I remember the stunning appearance of the first Zeppelin which tried to plant a few eggs (bombs) with little success on the city. There was the fully ineffective cannonade of the so-called anti-aircraft guns mounted on the Eiffel Tower, directed against the visiting acrid monster, lending to the excitement.' (*Beyond the Last Blue Mountain,* R.M. Lala)

JRD adds:'I was not interested in or understood the grim and bloody struggle in the trenches which took the flower of France's and Britain's youth, but the great deeds of the knights of the air fired me with enthusiasm and I remember one day complaining to my mother that if she had the good sense to marry my father five or six years earlier I could have been a fighter pilot too. I fervently hoped at least that the war would last long enough for me to become one!' (*Beyond the Last Blue Mountain,* R.M. Lala)

He further adds:'Oddly enough, some forty years later I was honoured, amongst other international airline bosses, with the French Legion of Honour. As our decorations were pinned on us by the then Minister for Aviation (who later became the Prime Minister of France for the usual short period) he addressed brief congratulatory remarks to each of us. When my turn came he said, "I shall not embarrass Mr. Tata by recalling his deeds of valour as a fighter pilot in the First World War." As I was only ten years old when the war started and fourteen when it ended, I was left with only two choices! Either to protest that I wasn't that hero—embarrassing the poor man in the process—or to be guilty of accepting an undeserved award. After about a second of mature consideration I accepted the decoration with as modest a mien as I could put on.' (*Beyond the Last Blue Mountain*, R.M. Lala)

Sooni was feeling a lot of pressure at one time. She had to devote considerable time in the service of medication at the hospital, and simultaneously had to nurture her family. Due to this overwhelming pressure, she contracted tuberculosis. In those days tuberculosis was an incurable disease, and patients battling this suffered the mental trauma of impending doom. Though Sooni's case was of the same category, but the nourishment she had, the measures she had taken and obviously the good climate helped her immensely. Then R.D. decided to set sail for India with his family. Though the seas were under tremendous natural as well as political turbulence, they reached India safely, and here started another new life of the immature, yet bright Jehangir.

❑

Damsel Dancing from East to West

Previously, when R.D. came to Bombay along with his family , he would rent a special house for them. But this time he did not go for that. The possible reason could be that he did not want to strain his wife in her illness. So he decided to take rooms of a suite at Taj Mahal Hotel, the megastar of Bombay hotel-residency. At that time, no other hotel could provide better comfort than that of the Jamsetji-built Taj. Sooni was under special care, nourished with unimaginable quality of food and else. JRD and his siblings were also under utmost care and provided the best of facilities.

But the change of climate from Paris to Bombay took a heavy toll on Sooni's health. Though all the facilities were there, but the ambience was not suitable for her health. In view of this, R.D. sent his family to Japan for specifically two reasons. The natural climate of Yokohama would easily resemble that of Paris' weather, and R.D. had very special trading relations with Japan.

Sooni and her children went there in 1917 and hired a big house. Sooni was impressed with the ambience and the warmth of the people of Japan. She travelled extensively throughout the country with her children. At this point, the inevitable impetus of formal education entered in their lives. JRD got admitted into a large Jesuit Boys' school of Yokohama, while his eleven-months-senior sister Sylla joined the Sacred Heart Convent School. The English school where JRD was admitted was run by American Jesuits and the impressions there left a significant impact on his childhood memories. Though they were very early days of his life, and for the first time he was experiencing life outside his homely premises, it was not the 'love at first sight' from his end. The way one day the teachers misbehaved with a fat Jewish boy JRD shocked JRD He recalls: 'They harassed the poor fellow. If he spoke out of turn they went out of their way to ridicule him. And I went out of my way to make friends with him because the other boys—mostly American—were anti-Semitic.' (*Beyond the Last Blue Mountain,* R.M. Lala)

JRD encountered a boy's first adolescent fantasy when he met his would-be first girlfriend there. He states: M. Lala'There was a French family in Yokohama. The father had come out to Japan as a young man with his wife. He was a businessman and he gradually built up a family of five children and so the children and we were there together. The eldest son was about my size and age. We were very good friends but the friendship did not last beyond the time in Japan.' (*Beyond the Last Blue Mountain*, R.M. Lala)

The daughter of that family was his first girl friend. He continues: R.M. Lala'She was eighteen and I was fourteen. It broke my fourteen-year-old heart when she married an officer from the French Tank Corps. I didn't know they even had tanks in those days. A wonderful woman anyway.' (*Beyond the Last Blue Mountain,* R.M. Lala)

In 1918, the Tata family bade Japan adieu, and set sail for India again. At that time the First World War was still raging. The vast ocean with the same wave ringing and drowning JRD was observing, where the adolescent boy never thought that the coast of this blue monstrous liquid was filled with the actual devils and the humanity and civilisation were priced high. (Author please simplify previous lines) His innocent fourteen-year old mind had no idea of the devastating war, but had the acquaintance of an old Remington machine in their ship Hirano Maru, and there he spent his time learning typing.

They disembarked at Colombo and the ship set sail for Britain amid the ongoing war. They had made some good friends on the Hirano Maru, and especially the captain and the purser. But after some weeks of their returning to India, they received devastating news, a bolt from the blue. *Hirano Maru* was bombarded on the English coast and sank within a few minutes, with the friends of the Tata family. This sudden disaster left a mark on poor JRD's mind, and who knows, from this news of mishap, JRD understood the power of destruction a war possesses.

Armistice was declared in November the same year. The opprobrious treaty of Versailles was to be signed between England-France axis and Germany. The following year, after the war having stopped, Sooni, along with her children, set sail for France again.

❑

Return to the Bed of Roses

When the family reached France, an obvious political turmoil was raging. After the moral win against the Germans, France was divided into two ideologies—one driven by Prime Minister Georges Clemenceau and the other by Marshal Foch. They were the two dominating saviours of the country in the First World War. But, after the victory, the clash soon began as the two tried to pull the country in two different ways, having no chance of reconciliation. At that time, the peace conference of Versailles was being held and unknowingly, Clemenceau was sowing the seeds of the Second World War and Hitler's imminent retaliation.

Jehangir was too young to understand the ideological conflict. He was only fifteen years then and had not done much reading. Here, he was admitted to Janson De Sailly, at least for the next five years till their next move. He recalls his school as: '...a very fine school, a great public school of Paris, but not in the British sense. It didn't have boarders but we were in the middle of the town, very near to where we lived, a hundred yards or so.' (*Beyond the Last Blue Mountain*, R.M. Lala)

He continues: 'In my class I had the reputation of being the fastest to run down the stairs and it was quite a long staircase we had in our school. I remember that in the French literature class I used to take pleasure in writing and perhaps I must have revealed some talent at it. I well remember our class in French literature, where the teacher used to call me for some strange reason, *L'Egyptien*. In front of me sat a big fat boy called Elkingon, a grandson of Napoleon's Marshal Ney. Our class had just written an imaginative piece on a subject given to us and I had written a very tearful story about how a woman's husband was killed in the war and how the poor lady was pursued by somebody. Announcing the results, the teacher walked down the centre aisle of the classroom. There were about 8 to 10 rows. The teacher said,

"You will be surprised to know that the competition last week was won by..." and he paused. He was looking past Elkingon to me. Elkingon thought he was the winner. He rose with a broad smile and started bowing, when the teacher brusquely told him "No, not you. Sit down. *L'Egyptien*—behind you." Poor chap!' (*Beyond the Last Blue Mountain,* R.M. Lala)

JRD was a naughty youngster and very fond of pranks too. In his words: 'I was up to a fair amount of mischief and played practical jokes on people and I think I inherited my sense of humour from my French grandfather. In those days people used to wear hard straw hats in summer. And a favourite prank of mine used to be to stand on the balcony of my house (or my friend's) above the street and wait for a passerby wearing one of these hats. Then we would drop a pea or a pellet onto his hat... ping!... and the person would jump up with a start and look all around to see who had done it. But we would duck and be out of sight. On one occasion, however, we did get into trouble. The person on whom we dropped a pellet, happened to be a professor from our school, whom we had not recognised. He pretended as if nothing had happened and walked on a little further. He crossed the street and watched us from the opposite side of the street. Then he came upstairs to complain. Of course we didn't answer the door... we were hiding in the lavatory!' (*Beyond the Last Blue Mountain,* R.M. Lala)

He continues: 'In those days there used to be pennies with holes in them. So we would tie a long white thread through the hole and wait for someone to pass by; when he did, we'd quickly lower the penny onto the pavement ...ping ... and whisk it up just as quickly. And the person would think some coins had fallen out of his pocket, so he'd stop, shuffle around in his pockets and look for the coins... which he never did find!' (Beyond the Last Blue Mountain, R.M. Lala)

When in later life he was asked whether he was an extraordinary student in his school, he recalled (in an issue of *Partha*, Bombay, September 1988.):

'I assume that I was reasonably intelligent... I was interested in politics and I was very much against foreign domination in India, but I didn't do anything about it. I was very interested in sports... hockey, football... every kind of sport. I wasn't interested in pretty girls then, I got interested in them much later. I found sports more interesting. But the real reason was that I was shy of girls. I had this impression that girls were silly, giggly persons. And girls used to make fun of boys. Girls also used to think that boys were stupid and this last bit, I believe is still correct!'

In those years in Janson De Sailly, Jehangir had two good friends. One was Louis Bleriot Jr, and the other Zent D'Alnoys. The meet with young Bleriot had a significant impact on Jehangir's life. Bleriot joined in pushing the aeroplanes in his father's hangar. His interest for aviation was tremendous. He loved the mechanical constructions of a flight and used to experiment with it. In 1927, when Charles Lindbergh was preparing for the first trans-Atlantic flight from New York to France, Bleriot was planning exactly the vice versa, to fly to America from France. In view of this, he also had built quite a bigger plane than that of Lindbergh's, but unfortunately was struck down with appendicitis and unexpectedly , passed away post-surgery.

In a Bleriot airplane, Jehangir experienced his first taste of aviation. He, who will be regarded as one of the masters in aviation, got his first opportunity to fly at that time, and obviously, through the doting support of his mother, Sooni. Every summer in post-war France, Tata family visited their home at 'plage d'Hardelot'. It was the site of the Field of the Cloth of Gold where one of the early summit talks took place between Henry VIII of England and Francis I of France. On that beach, one day a Bleriot airplane landed, to everyone's great excitement. JRD recalls: 'It was flown by his chief pilot, Adolphe Pegoud, the first man to loop-the-loop. Aeroplanes in those days did not have enough power or the driving speed to climb into a loop in what became the standard way later. So he did an outside loop! He just dived and kept pushing on the stick until he went all the way round, hanging on a belt!

A brave but foolhardy thing to do. It was a miracle the wings didn't come off! As a result Pegoud became world famous in aviation circles. Once, when he landed on the Hardelot beach he hit a soft spot, the plane went up on its nose and broke its wooden propeller. The propeller was afterwards cut and he autographed pieces which were given away as presents. I treasured one for years.' (Beyond the Last Blue Mountain, R.M. Lala)

Professional pilots at that time used to fly different airplanes in different regions, followed by a successful landing at various spots and they used to provide joy rides to regional youngsters. One day, Sooni had decided to give her children an experience of flying; and this time it was from an aeronautical viewpoint in a plane. Jehangir was the first to be selected, and strapped into the extra seat behind the pilot in the small two-seaters. Probably, from this experience, the seeds of aviation were being sowed in young Jehangir's mind, that later made him one of the most successful aviators of his time.

❑

Ship of Shift Finds no Shore

In 1922, R.D. again decided to shift his family to Bombay from France, but this time planning to send Jehangir England for higher studies. It was quite obvious as R.D. at that time was busy in the manufacture of Indian products specifically, which was Jamsetji's vision too; and if his family stayed with him, then it would be easier for him to maintain a healthy balance between his personal and professional life concurrently. The plan for sending Jehangir to England was acceptable to the participant too, as he himself had that wish, which he later confessed. By that time Sooni's health was deteriorating. The killer disease was unknowingly and silently eating her up from inside. R.D.'s mental agony was a million times higher than an examinee sitting in the first row thinking of how to manage to steal the answer copy of his friend. On the one hand, he was struggling to brush up Tata Steel, as a perfect competitor to what foreign steel had been, and on another hand he was fighting for the survival of Tata Industrial Bank. As he had only two hands, the news of Sooni's deteriorating health and the future of his next generation weighed heavy on his mind. In those days, there was no telephone connection and regular air travel to Europe directly from Bombay had not yet started. R.D. was in utter helplessness with all the problems, having no solution. Finally, after some days, a cable was delivered to him. The ultimate facsimile of human life, the life of his dearest, had arrived. (Author please explain previous line) Sooni had expired. Later, he gave his Malabar Hill house the name of his late wife. The house that he had planned to set up to take care of Sooni got the name, not the mistress herself. To quote from, '*Bonolota Sen*', by Jibanananda Das, "*pakhir nirer moto chokh tule bose ache" (Author please give English translation).* Sunita, the memorial of Sooni.

By the time R.D. reached France, Sooni was already buried. R.D. spent the next seven days in a whirlwind, finalised the preparations for his children to stay there, and he himself got back post-haste to save the Tata Industrial Bank; though, later, it did merge with Central Bank of India. In October, 1923, R.D. sent Jehangir to a crammer in England. The main purpose was to make him fluent in English prior to his admission to Cambridge. Jehangir was eager to carry on his career in Engineering.

The crammer was situated Southold, Suffolk, on the North Sea. It was one of the coldest parts of Eastern England. The school was to brush up him and other students to sit for the entrance examination of the university. The situation and ambience was tough for him as a complete outsider. Though there were other foreign students, but the upbringing of Jehangir was somehow restraining him from mingling wholeheartedly.. In spite of spending almost a year in England, he could not associate himself with the complexities of English and Western culture. He recalls in his own words: 'It was a fairly useful time. I worked. I learnt. I boxed. And on one occasion I froze. It was a bright summer day so all the boys were marched off for a swim. With gay abandon I jumped in. But the North Sea even in summer is freezing cold. I thought I would die.' (*Beyond the Last Blue Mountain*, R.M. Lala)

The bullying of an outsider is evident throughout history, and Jehangir was no exception. He was called "Frenchy" by the teachers, as his accent was not 'pure' in terms of

British pronunciation. He was constantly made fun of for his pronunciation. But one incident changed this scenario, and respect came to him quite unexpectedly from a boxing instructor of his school, who was an ex-Sergeant. Again, in his own words: 'He found me a bit reticent to use my right hand so one day he stuck his chin out and said, "Come on! Hit me!" I clipped him with my right. His eyes rolled up and he staggered back, held himself and said "That's enough." I discovered that though I was thin as a reed, I had a very good punch.' (With young boys one punch speaks louder than a barrage of words.) (*Beyond the Last Blue Mountain*, R.M. Lala)

Just when the crammer period got over and Jehangir was about to knock at the doors of Cambridge, a law was passed in France. All French boys at the age of twenty must serve the national army for two years mandatorily. The eldest of the family would get a concession and a no-objection, if he wished within the duration of a year. As a citizen of France, Jehangir had to join the French Army for at least a year and his dream of Cambridge had to be postponed for the following year, 1925. In between this time, he spent some holiday pastimes in his Bombay house.

Every good thing comes to an end, and so a holiday. His enjoyment in Bombay was coming to an end before returning to France to serve in their national army. He recapitulates: 'If I had to join the army, I wanted to pick the cavalry. I had seen polo matches in Bombay and Poona. Polo seemed a very exciting game and I thought maybe I could play polo later but first I had to learn to ride properly. So when the time came to go into the army I pulled strings to join the cavalry, not too successfully as it turned out. My grandmother spoke to a General she knew. To my consternation, I was drafted in an Algerian regiment, an Arab regiment, where riding was very different from normal riding. You ride Arab horses—very exciting horses—on a different kind of saddle. This saddle had a pommel in front and if you jerked forward the pommel hit you in the plexus. If the horse galloped forward and you were not prepared for it, you lurched back where the rear saddle hit and bounced you forward, sometimes over the head of the horse.' So, to his dismay, far from learning to ride well enough to play polo he was constantly anxious of being pierced by the high pommel in front or being catapulted over the head of the horse. 'When riding you leaned forward in the saddle rubbing a part of the bottom different from the one on a European saddle. Within the first two days I had blisters. The Sergeant told me that when I got up in the morning I should go and sit in the horse trough. And for two days I did. It felt like fire but cured it.' (*Beyond the Last Blue Mountain*, R.M. Lala)

The regiment was called *Le Saphis* (The Sepoys) and was composed of Algerians, Tunisians, Moroccans and a few French. It had the base-camp in an obscure city called Vienne, situated in the southern part of Lyon. Again, the initial feeling of crammer life coincided with the peculiarly enthusiastic feeling of serving the nation. Jehangir was brought up in luxury, but in his new surroundings he found nobody with whom he could match up. Everybody was alien to him in all terms, from manners to education, dressing-up to food habits. He felt trapped among some nomadic people, suddenly thrust in unhygienic and primitive conditions. He was shocked when he found that the soldiers did not go for a bath for a long time. Jehangir was the odd one out who went to a public bath at least twice in a week. The fellow soldiers used to make fun of him for his sophisticated nature and thought him to be a lunatic. Jehangir was absolutely clueless as to how to save himself before saving the nation.

Help always comes in unexpected ways. Here, Jehangir's Captain found him to be a well-educated prodigy who even knew typing. Jehangir recounts: 'The Captain, sporting the forbidding name of *Massacrer,* which in French literally means massacrer, promptly had me assigned as secretary in his office. One of the valued perquisites was that I did not have to get up at 5.30 in the morning to wash and groom my horse. The horse was ready for me. All I had to do was to climb the horse, sword in hand and exercise it. Another perk, so far as I was concerned, was that on my appointment to the good Captain's office, I was transferred from my highly redolent dormitory to a storeroom which I shared with an old Arab veteran called Guelool, who, unfortunately, smoked and coughed all night. I later discovered that the real reason for this transfer from the dormitory was to keep me out of sight for fear that I might be pinched by a higher regimental officer. It did not take long for the Colonel to find out that the First Squadron had an educated prodigy, who could not only read and write French and English but could even type. I was then transferred, for the second time, to the relatively luxurious office of the Colonel, and a bed was provided for me in a back room where I was gloriously alone.

'I became a favourite of officers applying for leave, whose applications I typed and who often graciously tipped me with a franc. During my year in the Saphis, I may have proved to be a good clerk, but I acquired little of military value for the possible defence of France. This was just 15 years before World War II broke out with its tanks and planes. We were given 6 rounds of ammunition, one live and five blanks. I fired a total of only 5 bullets. But I did learn to wield a sabre from horseback with reasonable proficiency. I remember feeling, and saying later, that if the Saphis were typical of France's Army, she would lose the next war. It nearly happened.' (*Beyond the Last Blue Mountain*, R.M. Lala)

At the end of his mandatory military service period, Jehangir came to know that an educated soldier volunteering for an extension of six months could get an opportunity to pursue an Officers' Training Course, and after that, was eligible to attend one of the world's most famous riding schools at Saumur. He decided to apply for one year's extension of his service. But here came the first clash between father and son. R.D. soon turned down his proposal angrily and informed him about his next future plan, to appoint Jehangir in their family business. Jehangir was upset butbowed to parental decision. But he got immensely shocked when he got to know that to keep his father's choice, he could not complete his dream Cambridge degree too, as it was not essential for his future association with Tatas. He never protested that time but later confessed in an interview with R.M. Lala, his most authentic biographer, "…this decision is one I've regretted throughout my life and which caused me to have a long-lasting inferiority complex.'

Immersing his dream in the water of earthly solitude of suspense, (Author please simplify) in December, 1925, Jehangir landed in India and started his new career as an unpaid apprentice in Tata.

❑

The Bubbles of Dissertation

In Bombay, Jehangir could enjoy a season of comfort after the hectic life as a soldier in France. Here, life was fast, aristocratic and most importantly, fitted Jehangir's mindset. Earlier memories of Bombay were naturally not registered in his mind very minutely, but this time he looked for the new city with great enthusiasm and was eager to work. Here, he persuaded his father, who bought his first Bugatti, which was blue in colour. He used to take his father for a ride and R.D. also enjoyed the outings. Not only this, Jehangir also practised shooting with a rifle. As recounted by Zal Taleyarkhan, one of Jehangir's earliest companions in Bombay, they would hunt crows and vultures. The life was very energetic as well as entertaining for Jehangir; this on the one hand relieved his earlier stress of army life, and on the other hand, was preparing him for his upcoming service.

The relationship between father and son was also a matter of interest. As we observed earlier, there was a slight psychological clash between them, though one-sided, for Jehangir obeyed his father wholeheartedly; their relationship clarified one point, and that was steadfast character, a legacy of their great predecessor Jamsetji Tata. R.D. in his own life was very punctual and laborious in nature, for everyday he would reach his office before anybody appeared and cleared up his desk and other equipment single-handedly. About his father, Jehangir said: 'Father was a great tease, so we never knew what prank he would be up to. One day we were at the Ripon Club, where he had a lot of Parsee cronies. A friend was taking a drink at the dining table when R.D. smacked him from behind and the poor man spluttered on the table. There was almost a brawl. Then there was a dentist friend of father's who had palsy and his hands shook. Father went round loudly proclaiming he had pulled out the wrong tooth! A kind of childishness but he was good company.' (*Beyond the Last Blue Mountain*, R.M. Lala)

He continued by saying that R.D. was: '…very charming, a totally open, honest kind of man. He had no kind of pride in him. He was very unlike Sir Dorab who was pompous. R.D. spoke French, had lived in China, and was cosmopolitan.' JRD was fond of his father and admired, him but, 'we never had time for a close and leisurely relationship. Father was not a great but a select eater. He loved French wine. Once he came home, he threw away all care and over the weekends I don't remember him doing what I always do, having a box full of papers to clear.' (B*eyond the Last Blue Mountain,* R.M. Lala)

At that time, Jehangir, a twenty-year-old youth, used to visit the steel city, i.e., Jamshedpur with his father and paid visits to the Director's Bungalow. With a great future vision, R.D. used to include him in their discussions and paid attention to Jehangir if he had anything to say. This was his first experience on his way to becoming one of the most successful scions of the Tata empire.During Jehangir's slow but steady involvement with their family business, and he was gradually becoming aware of his historical lineage. Tata Steel was suffering a blow that was directly connected with India's Freedom Movement. In 1924, the Steel Industry Protection bill was introduced on the recommendation of Tariff Board. This was a historic decision, as through this bill, the British Government would protect the Tatas' manufacture at their expense. It was quite obvious that the Indians would oppose it; as with this, the empirical motion of Britishers would get strengthened with the furnished hand of Indian industry, the single firm to represent the production of steel in India. But Motilal Nehru supported the bill, though rejecting the proposal of becoming the chief of the Select Committee. Chaman Lai and N.M. Joshi had not supported the bill, saying that if Britishers came to take care of Indian industry, why did they not directly nationalise the industry and so did not confirm the security of the workers.(Author please check previous sentence for clarity) Amidst the huge confusion, the bill was passed in a voice vote. Tatas never wanted the Government to take over the company, for their sole intention was to run the industry through their own infrastructure and investment. R.D. did not support the bill anyhow, but others were recommending him to yield to the British. Again, to slay the slain, an earthquake shook Japan, the Tatas' major customer of pig iron. Tatas were suffering huge financial loss; even Sir Dorab had to pledge his entire personal belongings towards a loan of twenty million rupees.

Misfortune does not come alone. It is true and was proven from the above scenario. However, misfortune always comes with a hidden ray of hope, of upcoming fortune. That came to the frame at that moment. By the end of the year 1924, the positive effect of that bill was gradually appearing, obviously thanks to the Extension Programme, and the outcomes of the Steel Protection Act were also visible and the Tatas survived.Then, one man entered the scene, which would later play an important role in Jehangir's grooming. R.D. requested John Peterson to be appointed as the Director-in-charge of Tata Steel. Previously Peterson was Director of Munitions at the time of the First World War and met R.D., who was supplying military artifacts and steel rails on behalf of Tata Steel. The duo became so close, that on one request of R.D., he appointed himself in the said post. R.D. then introduced Jehangir to Peterson and gave him (Peterson) the responsibility to look after him. As Jehangir recalls of that time: 'Peterson never had a moment of privacy. Every single paper going to his desk was routed through me. I studied it before I sent it up. And I studied his comments before I sent them out. I must say that was a very formative and important time of my career, when I saw how a highly trained ICS administrator worked. I learnt a lot from that.' (Beyond the Last Blue Mountain, R.M. Lala)

After a few months of experience with Peterson, R.D. advised Jehangir to have some real experience of the workings of Tata Steel at Jamshedpur. In early 1926, Jehangir caught the train to Jamshedpur. This was his first step to encounter the visuals in his mind and he was excited. By this time, he had gone through a book called *Jamsetji Nusserwanji*

Tata—A Chronicle of his Life by F.R. Harris. This virtual meet with Jamsetji Tata aroused Jehangir's interest in their family business highly and he gradually was getting the glimpse of the marrow of the bone. Through this book, and the first-hand experiences related to him by his father, the heritage of the House of Tatas came alive for Jehangir, now, JRD

❑

Droplets of Dream Beyond the Limit

JRD's journey to Jamshedpur had imperial overtures (Author please explain imperial overtures) in the annals of history. Just the previous year, Gandhiji had visited the place and installed a wooden 'charkha', removing all the British accessories there. JRD's visit was exactly two decades after the man of steel, Jamsetji, had come across and established the infrastructure. The Tatas was no less than an empire, where one would form and the successors would reform and enliven the whole. (Author please simplify) Jamsetji made the blue-print and unveiled the new hope of industry, followed by Dorab, R.D., and JRD continuing the legacy till now.

Upon arrival at Jamshedpur, he shared a bungalow with J.K. Sondhi, the Town Administrator, Jehangir (called Joe) Ghandy, who later became the first Indian General Manager of the company and Joe's brother, Dinshaw (called Dinsi) Ghandy. Dinsi was the boss. With them, he was gettinga first-hand experience of the company's workings, and understood the practicalities rather than mere objective theories. He had gone through a book called The Shaping and Making of Steel and according to that he used to visit every unit and department there.

While he was learning the ropes wholeheartedly, R.D. went to France that summer to spend some time with his other children; that was his final visit to France. He passed away there after a massive cardiac arrest and overnight the Tatas became fatherless. The news came to JRD via telegram but unfortunately, he could not go to attend his father's funeral as Imperial Airways had no proper route (preferable, Karachi to London). He recalls after his father's collapse: 'Though he was 70, to me he was a man who still had 20 years left in him. I had no inkling that I was not going to see him around but he seemed to have had a premonition about his death otherwise he would have allowed me to go to Cambridge and get a degree of some kind. 'I remember him for his spendthriftness, no, it's a wrong word—generosity. He was always helping people, giving out money, spending money, building this white elephant, "Sunita", a beautiful house. So, although I am left with the impression of a very fine man, I would have liked to have known him more closely. We were separated so much of the time. It was always a joy to get together again but it didn't last very long.' (*Beyond the Last Blue Mountain*, R.M. Lala)

Now, JRD had the huge responsibility to run the business and the family simultaneously. Just at the age of twenty-two, he found himself the head of the family. But he had by then faced the actual scenario, full of complexities and sufferings. He was not an outsider to India, but lacked proper cultural bonding. He had been schooled in different countries and never had lived in a particular country for a long time. He had no trustworthy friend or relative, and his 'Frenchy' nature was more prominent than that of an Indian. Moreover, he did not have a clear idea about the financial background at that time. Though Sir Dorab was there, but he had so much pressure of running the company in different directions that he could not focus much on the Jamshedpur factory. And to top it all, in his last years, R.D. was absorbed in the workings of Tata Sons and his other foreign private companies had been neglected.

JRD's first priority was to pay off the debts; R.D. had borrowed money from Sir Dorab at different times. He sold their home "Sunita" and moved to a suite at the Taj Mahal Hotel. The property of Hardelot was also sold and finally what remained were the shares in the company, a third of the total. JRD recalls later: 'It was a difficult period, because I did not have the background or experience. The Will said that I should get the first Rs 3,000 a month, Dorab Rs 2,000 a month, Jimmy Rs 1,000 a month and then what was left should be divided among the five of us. In fact, I would have got, think, the first Rs 3,000 or Rs 2,500 and nobody would have got anything else at all. But we sorted it out easily. I remember consulting father's old friend Dinshaw Daji. He said, of course you could do what you like if you all (brothers and sisters) agree. So, we ignored the Will. I decided the family income would be divided equally—l/5th each, including the shares. That was that.' (*Beyond the Last Blue Mountain,* R.M. Lala)

The debts were soon paid off. JRD started his working as the permanent Director of Tata Sons, a post that he had inherited from his father, and the company granted him a salary of Rs. 750 per month.

Soon after his father's demise, JRD was struck by bouts of typhoid and paratyphoid. But then, he had no time to rest much. He had to work a lot to keep the balance of his company. He recalled later several times that he was ashamed of himself to be called by others as "uneducated", or "semi-educated". In India, where the academic currencies are the most efficient factors to consider a person's ability, it was quite obvious for JRD to listen to that. Even sixty years later, he blamed R.D. exclusively for not letting him study at Cambridge in his teens. He has admitted later, that only parental lineage and the history of ancestors had driven him to work for the company: 'Honestly, if I had not been the son of R.D. Tata or the son of one of the main Tatas, I don't think I would have been so driven. I was driven by the fact that there was Jamsetji Tata in my life and so that is what urged me to do things to justify myself. I was very doubtful about my own capacity to follow these people. I had great admiration for my father, little for Dorabji Tata, enormous for Jamsetji Tata and what Tatas meant.' (*Beyond the Last Blue Mountain*, R.M. Lala)

In those early days, John Peterson had mostly influenced and encouraged JRD on how to handle a business proficiently. He was the only man whom JRD followed quite blindly. JRD recalls: 'Peterson was one of the very rare people I respected both as a man and as one with an educated brain. There are very few men I know like that. He became a kind of father to me. It is from him I acquired many qualities like clearing papers with speed, passion for perfection. I know that aiming at perfection has its drawbacks. It makes you go into details you can avoid. It takes a lot of energy but that is the only way you can achieve excellence. So, in that sense, being finicky is essential.' (*Beyond the Last Blue Mountain,* R.M. Lala)

One thing that was of some discomfort to him was his French identity. His mother-tongue was French, and so his citizenship. He had realised that his place of working was India; and to work more efficiently, he had to renounce his French citizenship and his place in the French Army. He then wrote to the Ministry of Justice, Paris, in 1929 to set the papers to sever his French connection. Legally it was much easier than to sever culturally, though. For him, he had to switch his writing from French to English. In an interview with R.M. Lala, he recalls what Peterson had advised:

'As I did very little dictating in those days, I used to write by hand. Then Peterson said, "Look, you must get into the habit of dictating otherwise one takes more time." Some people can't dictate at all and I certainly couldn't (in English.) I was terrified of dictating. So, I'd send for Iyer to take a letter and read out from a letter I'd already written and concealed from view beneath the table, to give myself confidence.'

Gradually he took hold of the office in his strict hands, which he inherited from his parental lineage, and headed the affairs with ease. Then at one point of time, he met with an accident, for which he had to appear in court. Eventually the case was dismissed, but he had to sell his first Bugatti. During this time, another accident took place in his life; a clash of two eyes! JRD was lovestruck after meeting Thelma, a niece of Jack Vicaji, a top criminal lawyer of that time. Thelma Vicaji became JRD's wife on 23 December, 1930. The young couple chose Darjeeling as their honeymoon destination, and both spent a happy married life. On the one hand, he had the Tata office, circulated throughout the world, (Author please explain circulated) on another hand he had his family to take care of, and finally had a married life to nurture. Besides, he had his self-esteem of a cultural silhouette. (Author please explain previous line) JRD became successful to carry his entire world till the last day of his life.

The Tatas were so successful through their flourishing business of Tata Steel that they started to spread their wings in different fields, right from sugar to electro-chemicals, construction and what not! And it was not matter of joke that they succeeded in every line. They attempted to initiate technological support in the 1920s to their company to increase the power of production. The companies executed outstanding constructional works such as the Vaitarna Dam and several long railway bridges across the Indus, the Godavari, the Krishna and the Narmada rivers. JRD was a proud participant in some of these large projects and witnessed how their company used to work in different situations. Apart from R.D., the one who was at once the saviour and one of the driving forces (Author please give better phrase for engine forces) of the Tatas was Sir Dorab. The way Bairam Khan assisted Humayun, and after his death, took care of young Akbar, Sir Dorab too helped R.D. in many ways, one was obviously the sacrifice of his entire personal wealth, and also after the death of him, and he was the guardian of Tatas and guide of young JRD He had also founded a trust in Tatas' welfare, and funded India's first super-speciality cancer hospital, the Tata Memorial. His trust also funded the establishment of Tata Institute of Social Sciences (TISS), the Tata Institute of Fundamental Research (TIFR) and the National Centre for the Performing Arts. JRD was a trustee of this trust from its very outset in 1932.

Although the company had been doing well, probably with God's blessings, at each and every tumbling point, one remained always ready beforehand to take the baton and direct the motion in a righteous way. JRD was like a fortunate middle-order batsman who had to just carry out the legacy of his earlier big-shots. He did that promptly, but alongside he also initiated some other ways to hit boundaries forming his unique wagon-wheel. And from this time, he began to explore his innovative abilities and amplified his vision beyond the horizon.

❑

Love of the Life: Aviation

The Tata group of companies was founded by Jamsetji Tata in 1868 and has been reigning for over one hundred and fifty years. It seems like a dynasty is ruling and JRD Tata is the rightful heir of Jamsetji Tata.The 'Father of Indian Industry' Jamsetji Tata built India's biggest conglomerate. JRD Tata too possessed these qualities similar to his great ancestor Jamsetji and started a new era of Tata group of companies.

Jehangir Ratanji Dadabhoy Tata or mostly known as JRD Tata despite being an important member of the Tata family had his own passion different from the industrial field. But unlike other privileged people of a royal family who can destroy the whole family business to follow their passion, JRD channelled his passion to the right way and started another new spectrum of business. His passion, which was aviation, proved to be a wonderful sector that helped the business of Tata group of companies to flourish enormously.

Jehangir always had a passion for aviation and he even was India's first-ever licensed pilot. He even flew the first commercial flight. But he did not limit his passion by flying only commercial flights. He, just like his forefather Jamsetji, had a bigger plan for the Tata group. The existing chairman of Tata Sons was Dorab Tata at that point of time. His enthusiasm to invest in an airline was very low but JRD's mentor persuaded Sir Dorabji to agree on this matter. Soon, the Tatas started flying airplanes carrying mail from Mumbai to Karachi, without even having a proper setup. There was insufficient space to take off or land a plane in Mumbai so they had to use the mudflats in Juhu. But JRD, being a trained pilot and a confident man, completed this adventure very smoothly. This was definitely a big milestone in JRD Tata's life and also for their future airlines.

Once he said cherishing this moment, 'On an exciting October dawn in 1932, a Puss Moth and I soared joyfully from Karachi with our first precious load of mail, on an inaugural flight to Bombay. As we hummed towards our destination at a "dazzling" hundred miles an hour, I breathed a silent prayer for the success of our venture and for the safety of those who would work for it. We were a small team in those days. We shared successes and failures, the joys and heartaches, as together we built up the enterprise which later was to blossom into Air-India and Air-India International.' (*Beyond the Last Blue Mountain,* R.M. Lala)

The hard work of the Tatas in the aviation sector soon brought the attention of the Directorate of Civil Aviation or the DCA for their remarkable punctuality even in the months of monsoon. This consistency gained a remarkable review from the DCA: 'As an example of how an airmail service should be run, we commend the efficiency of Tata Services who on October 10, 1933, arriving at Karachi as usual on time, completed a year's working with 100% punctuality... even during most of the difficult monsoon months when rainstorms increased the perils of the Western Ghats portion of the route no mail from Madras or Bombay missed connection at Karachi nor was the mail delivered late on a single occasion at Madras . . . our esteemed trans-Continental Airways, alias Imperial Airways, might send their staff on deputation to Tatas to see how it is done.' (Beyond the Last Blue Mountain, R.M. Lala)

This service was completely on the Tatas without any sort of government aid even after asking for it. But during this tough time, JRD showed consistent endurance as a bridge between the company and the government. The initial response of the government was not very ideal for the Tatas as personal flying had a stigma of being a pleasure of the privileged people. But JRD was a visionary who knew that flying would receive much more importance than just carrying mails.

JRD had a prior clear sense that the aviation industry would enrich the Tata company for the future prospect as well. From 1933 with the mail delivering process, the initiation of the Tata Airlines started. The initial days were difficult for the pilots but this service never stopped. After Sir Nowroji passed away in 1938, Jehangir Ratanji Dadabhoy Tata was the next chairman of the Tata group of companies. After he became the chairperson, with time the growth of Tata Airlines increased, and the first-ever enterprise between the public and private sector was made in India.

JRD has always wanted the government to invest in Tata's airlines and in this regard he had quite a few discussions with the British government. But no fruitful result was found. But in 1947 when India was experiencing its freedom, JRD envisioned a new chance of a relationship between the government and Tata Airlines. He proposed to the government an equity holding of 49 percent of the capital of Tata Air Lines, kept 25 percent for the company and shared the rest publicly. Later on, the government bought an extra 2 percent and rightfully became the controlling power of Tata Air Lines. With a new name Air-India was formed, a joint enterprise between the government and the Tatas.

JRD was not only a man interested in expanding his business but also was a man who strictly believed in proper training to attain skills. His focus was always on how his pilots and workers could be trained in a better way to handle tough and unfavourable situations. This personality trait of JRD was found to be very helpful during communal violence in Punjab and West Bengal after the independence of India. During this troublesome period, many volunteers were rushing to these places to help out the suffering people. Among them, the team that performed really efficiently was the team from the Institute of Social Sciences (TISS), Bombay.

The efficient workers of this team gained a special appreciation from Prime Minister Jawaharlal Nehru, 'We found the difference in their (TISS team) work and the work of many others who were earnest and who had done their best but who did not have the training to do it well. There is a difference between the trained workers and the merely enthusiastic workers.' (*J.R.D: TATA THE MAGIC OF LEADERSHIP*, Cyrus M. Gonda)

JRD was also very particular regarding the quality of the equipment needed for a plane. In the initial times, the engines of planes were made by a British company called Pratt and Whitney. The 707 engines made by this company were definitely very competent. But JRD still had doubts about these engines and wanted to research deeply as to which company made the best engines for airplanes. He found out that Rolls-Royce Conway engines were the best among all the other engines for airplanes and contacted Boeing for these customised engines. JRD Tata's decision of changing the engines influenced many other airlines in America as well.

A small incident regarding these two engines confirms the farsighted nature of JRD. IndiGo, that is India's largest carrier, uses the engines of Pratt and Whitney. They have faced several problems during the grounding of the aircraft creating problems for the passengers. But the Rolls-Royce engine has no such problem and is very efficient. This shows how deep a knowledge and wise a judgment JRD Tata had even when most people thought otherwise. This incident is not totally connected with JRD but it definitely shows his right vision that is undefeatable even in the present times. (Author please explain why not connected to JRD)

❑

New Beginning as Chairman

Jehangir Ratanji Dadabhoy Tata started a new era of business after he became the chairperson of the Board of Tata Sons. JRD who was very much occupied with his passion and other stuff was all at once the chairman after Sir Nowroji's sudden demise in 1938. JRD himself admits that he was not at all prepared for this sudden burden of so many responsibilities. The co-directors appointed JRD Tata as the new chairman because there was no other option at that point of time. Even JRD admits that it was not like he was capable of handling things and yet the co-directors chose him.

Once in an interview with R.M. Lala, JRD Tata without any hesitation admitted, 'Perhaps they preferred me to Sorabji Saklatvala (Jamsetji's nephew) who was old and not too bright.' Later on, his opinion changed and he thought about the decision of making him the chairman differently: 'I was appointed Chairman probably because I was the only surviving Director of Tatas (other than Lady Tata) who was permanent under the firm's constitution, and I presume I had made some mark on them. I did not have a high opinion of myself then nor do I even now, except that I am now recognised.'

However irrespective of what the reason was behind this decision, JRD proved himself very much worthy for holding that super important position in a huge company like Tata. Many questioned his capabilities at that time and Ardeshir Dalal, the first Indian to be Municipal Commissioner of Bombay was one of them. He thought of JRD as an ignorant person who will only be ruining the family business single-handedly. But JRD with his hard work and endless attempts to figure out the business proved Dalal wrong.

Tata Sonsconsisted of a whole lot of business sectors that were completely new to JRD. Initially, he felt very clueless about what to do or how to do. Understanding everything within a few days is next to impossible for any human being and JRD too was noexception. But JRD had something unique in him that made him take a big decision which his predecessors would have never thought of. He in fact mentioned that he would not be rushing from one meeting to another without knowing anything properly like his predecessors. That is reason he took a huge decision of giving up the chairmanship of certain companies because the pressure was huge to take on.

JRD never over-estimated himself just because his last name was next to royalty. He understood that there were many able people who could handle the chairmanship of companies well. He gave up his chairmanship to an able man, Sir Homy Modi. JRD held on to the companies that he thought as his strength based on his knowledge, like—aviation, steel, etc.

He had a completely different thought process but as we all know our predecessors still have some kind of influence upon us. Similarly, the great Jamsetji Tata influenced the house of Tata to hold that strong and unique position in a nation like India where royal names are not very rare to find. His principles, beliefs, and vision towards the business inspired everyone in the Tata family. JRD too started absorbing the principles and beliefs of his great-grandfather Jamsetji. Jamsetji Tata always used to prioritise the need of his nation and its people. The famous thing he used to say was 'What does the nation need?' According to the nation's need, Jamsetji and his company would function.

JRD got really inspired by this thought process and started to act likewise. 'What is good for India is good for the Tatas—this was the prime belief of JRD and his business strategies. JRD admired Jamsetji and his intelligence and vision a lot. Jamsetji once said, 'We do not claim to be more unselfish, more generous or more philanthropic than other people. But we think we started on sound and straightforward business principles, considering the interests of the shareholders our own, and the health and welfare of the employees the sure foundation of our prosperity.' These wise words of Jamsetji had a great impact on JRD and his later ventures.

JRD as a chairman had the first responsibility to tie the members of his company not only together but also unitedly. The Tata group had people as the board members who were almost double the age of JRD. Also, JRD's other family members were part of this big fat company. That is why tying everyone together was very important so that the company could run smoothly without having any internal problems. To build an empire and run it for long, it was very much needed to knit the members together; and JRD with his affection, respect, and friendship tried to gain that trust of his fellow members. This offering of friendship and respect was the foundation of JRD having such loyal team members as Sir Homi Mody.

Their friendship was beyond their professional relationship in the Tata group. In his farewell in the Tata group, Sir Homi Mody said about JRD, 'He has a very keen intellect, a little too keen. His versatility is truly amazing. Whether it is a blast furnace or an ice-cream freezer, an aircraft engine, or a cigarette lighter, he is equally at home with all of them. He affects to be his own doctor and a damned bad patient. All in all, I have great admiration and affection for our chairman, and I think Tatas are singularly fortunate in having as their Chief a man of such wide vision and such a fine sense of right and wrong.' The generous words of Sir Homi Mody show how beautifully JRD Tata had gained the faith of his team members.

❑

Creation of the Famous Bombay Plan

JRD Tata always considered the condition of India and the people living in it as a very important part of his business. During World War II, JRD was very sure that the British government will be destroyed economically; and that even if India does not gain independence, still the British government will be very much incapable to provide for the expenses of the Indian people. JRD had always a keen interest towards not only contemporary history but also ancient Roman and

Greek history. This interest and learning of history helped him to understand that India's independence was not very far to achieve. He understood the fact that after reclaiming their independence, Indian people will be needing some economical plan to sustain their lives without any difficulties.

Keeping all these things in mind, JRD and some other reputed industrialists decided to form a plan named the 'Bombay Plan'. The industrialists who joined JRD in this venture were—G.D. Birla; Kasturbhai Lalbhai, the textile mill owner from Ahmedabad; Sir Purshotamdas Thakurdas from Bombay and Sir Shri Ram from Delhi. All these industrialists thought to make a practical plan for the economic structure of India. This plan was published in two parts in the years 1943 and 1944. This plan is historic for India because it was the very first time where industrialists made a plan for the Indian economic, industrial and societal future.

It aroused a kind of a patriotic feeling among them and swiftly bashed the British rulers. The main agenda of the plan was to focus on the standard of living of the average Indian people after getting independent. The planners not only focused on the theoretical aspect but also made it a practical one considering many important aspects. They considered different aspects such as—volume and quantum of cloth, grain, housing, educational institutes, etc.

JRD once said about this plan, 'I can't take credit for more than being the first businessman to see the need for a Plan. It went on to planning but it started with a feeling that Indian businessmen must prepare themselves for what was to happen after the war . . . when India became free as I was sure it would and we must do something to develop the country. It was (to start with) only a committee of businessmen . . . (I thought) there must be a role for us—we must accelerate development, then in the course of deliberations came the idea of planning in the modern sense . . . I knew Independence was bound to come: I knew the country's economy would have to be tackled—that economic prosperity needed to reach not only the few but the many. Businessmen and not only the Government should play a role.' (*Beyond the Last Blue Mountain,* R.M. Lala)

There was definitely debate against this plan. Some Leftist people believed it to be a reactionary plan whereas some businessmen having old thoughts saw it as a radical one. But all these problems were solved with the help of the Economics and Statistics Department built up by the Tatas. JRD always had an interest in statistics of various things and this interest helped the Bombay Plan to get successful. With the help of this department, it was easy to set a target by the committee. Even though having a foolproof plan, it lacked in certain important areas like how to control the population growing day by day. JRD had talked about the fact that having too many people led to needing extra food or clothes or a place to live. But it is strange that despite talking about these factors, JRD paid very little attention to population control.

In spite of having much statistical information and opinions of leading industrialists, the Bombay Plan could not achieve the desired goal that the planners had thought. The major problem of this plan was that it had the least focus on agriculture. India being a country where nearly half of the population is engaged in agriculture needed more investment in this area. But unfortunately, the Bombay Plan only recommended ten percent to agriculture which was very little. JRD later accepted that it was their fault not to consider agriculture as an important area. Even though this plan failed but the importance of this plan as the very first initiative towards the betterment of Indian people cannot be denied at all. The capitalist world thinking about the economy of a country was definitely setting an example at that point of time.

❑

The Season of Rivalry with Birla

The top two names in the history of Indian industry for almost half a century in the time period before independence were—JRD Tata and G.D. Birla. These two have reigned the business industry with their intelligence and dedication towards their work. Even though they were not the best of friends which is very common, they still had certain respect towards each other. The first time the Birlas and the Tatas came together was for the Bombay Plan in the middle of the 1940s. But still, there were very rare occasions when these two would meet.

The Tatas were a business house established earlier, and had been reigning for a long period of time. There were some very evident differences between the two topmost businessmen. Starting from family background to upbringing to educational background, everything was the opposite except for one fact—their dedication towards business. An amazing fact of the Birlas was the rapid growth of their companies that was unstoppable. Starting with some twenty companies in the year 1945, the Birlas kept on growing. And by 1965 they were the owners of approximately two hundred companies. G.D. Birla was much influenced by the great Mahatma Gandhi and helped the Congress party a lot. But still, it did not affect his business in British-ruled India.

The two companies were expanding their business without harming each other but, during the year 1946, there was a conflict of interest between JRD and G.D Birla. The formation of a new airline was envisaged and, the Minister of Civil Aviation was issuing licenses liberally. JRD Tata had a great vision for his business and easily made out that it would create a danger for his airlines. G.D. Birla was very much interested in starting a new airline named Bharat

Airways, and even tried to tempt five trained pilots of the Tatas.

This was the beginning of a rivalry and JRD once wrote to G.D. Birla 'Apart from the general aspects of the question, I am even more sorry to find that Bharat Airways have been making a determined attempt at enticing some of our staff, and particularly our senior pilots, to join their organisation. I am sure you will agree that we have ground for considering this a most unfriendly act. In view of our friendly personal relations in the past, I do not believe that this step has been taken with your approval.' (*Beyond the Last Blue Mountain,* R.M. Lala)

This conflict and exchange of letters went on for over one year and after 1948 the relationship between G.D. Birla and JRD cooled. The fears of JRD regarding his airlines turned out to be true, but there was nothing much he could do. But the rivalry never went too far. After the demise of G.D. Birla, JRD paid his heartfelt tributes, 'Although I had known Mr. Birla for some fifty years, we met only at relatively rare intervals and to my regret our mutual relationship was therefore not a very close one…Although he was the product of a highly orthodox social and family environment in which he was born nearly ninety years ago, he had a remarkable combination of both a Cartesian Western mind and a traditional Hindu mind steeped in Hindu religion and philosophy. He must also have had a marvellously flexible mind for he was able to approach problems and issues with both parts of his mind and come up with practical solutions that compromised neither.'

❑

Legacy of Tisco and Many More

Tata Iron and Steel Company or TISCO was founded by the great Jamsetji Tata and later was established by Sir Dorabji Tata in 1907. It was 1911, when this company started expanding and also started producing boilers and locomotives. It was definitely a huge company having huge goals, providing the necessary things to the nation as well as to the workers.It was the first ever company in India that provided the policy of leave-with-pay. Having such high standards, it easily became the soft target of strike. There were continuous periods of workers starting a strike against the company. Even Mahatma Gandhi once had to come and request the workers to withdraw the strike and work peacefully. JRD once in a meeting with the board members said that the communication gap between the management and the workers is the main reason of this continuous saga of strikes.

JRD having this great vision and sense about business easily understood the fact that the management of Tata Steel needed to be considerate towards the workers and to listen to the workers as well. JRD himself was in a great relationship with the president of the Tata Steel Workers' Union Abdul Bari. Bari was a very ill-tempered and fiery person but JRD had a great respect towards Abdul Bari because of his honesty. They both had a mutual respect towards each other and their relationship grew keeping aside the problems of the company. Even though Bari's unfortunate death ended their friendship quicky, JRD never misjudged Bari for being a violently emotional person. He, in an interview with R.M. Lala, even said about Bari:

'I have told you of this little episode merely to illustrate my conviction that there is really no difficulty in establishing good relations with people in general and between Management and workers and their Union in particular if one cultivates a liking for, and trust in, those one deals with.'

JRD's business vision could figure out that his personal attempt to have a better relationship with the workers would not help the company in general. Everyone in the board of management needed to have that communication with the workers so that the work in the company could run smoothly. He wanted to build a Personnel Department in Tata Steel which was very bold of him as not many companies during that period of time thought about having a good communication with their workers. It was in 1947 that this department was established in Tata Steel; and it is still working as the bridge between the workers and the management.

This initiative of JRD helped the company when the issue of nationalising Tata Steel was raised for the second time, after the Indira Gandhi regime trying to nationalise Tata Steel in the year 1971. It was in the year 1979 when again the proposal of nationalising Tata Steel and some other companies was raised by two Cabinet Ministers of the Janata Government—George Fernandes and Biju Patnaik. These two were the ministers of Industries and Steel. But the Union of Tata Steel that was protesting and striking against its own management, protested against this proposal of nationalisation. It was the Union of Tata workers that first presented a petition to Prime Minister Morarji Desai. The

Tata Workers' Union of mines, steel plants, and collieries came together to protest against this injustice even before the management of the Tatas.

It was the love and respect that JRD had gained by communicating with the workers that helped him and the whole company to overcome this great issue of nationalisation. The fact that later in the year 1979 the whole company celebrated fifty long years of industrial harmony shows how to hold the workers in the team. JRD Tata, cherishing his experience with his workers, once in 1985 said to the people of Jamshedpur:

'I claim no personal credit for the outstandingly good and cooperative relations which have prevailed within the Company since those early days. If credit is due to any person in the Company for what has been achieved by these very means, it would be to your present Chairman, Mr. Russi Mody, whose human qualities and extraordinary ability to arouse love and friendship in others have been a source of inspiration to all, including myself. Cooperation is never a one-way traffic. From the Union we have in Mr. Gopal, a worthy successor to the traditions of Abdul Bari and Michael John, and we all admire the manner in which he is carrying the torch.

On the Management side Russi Mody's role in shaping industrial relations has been the most outstanding. When he was in the collieries, he established a unique rapport with the workers. Whenever he saw that there was a need or an injustice which the company could set right, he promptly acceded to the demand of the workers and when the line had to be held, he would hold it.' (*Beyond the Last Blue Mountain,* R.M. Lala)

Tata Steel was blooming in a full-fledged manner; and it also started manufacturing boilers and locomotives as well as road rollers, diesel engines, tractors, earthmoving equipment, etc. JRD could very well envision that post-war India would need these things and, there would be a high demand for them. Tatas were a prime company, and looked at as the ideal of any new project. JRD not only expanded Tata Steel brilliantly but also established a new branch—Tata Engineering and Locomotive Company or TELCO. During this period, JRD came across Sumant Moolgaokar who was then working with the Associated Cement Companies (ACC). Moolgaokar was a sharp man having knowledge about business and that is why he was successful in attracting the attention of JRD without even trying very hard. Sumant Moolgaokar joined the Tatas in the year 1949 as the Director-in-charge in TELCO.

The initial years of TELCO were not very smooth and were filled with ups and downs. The first orders the company used to get were mostly of building boilers.

The job was pretty hard and that is why the Pathans of the North-West were appointed to do the job. But with India gaining independence and the subsequent riots between Hindu and Muslims, all the Pathan workers fled to Pakistan almost handicapping the boiler plant. Moolgaokar trained the next crew of workers to get accustomed to the manufacturing process of the boilers. But the industry of boilers and locomotives was not very secure for the Tatas until Daimler-Benz contacted the Tatas.

Daimler-Benz was a company that manufactured trucks but did not expand its business outside of Germany. It was in 1950 that this company contacted Tatas and proposed a partnership of manufacturing trucks for them. The negotiation between the two companies took place in Geneva; JRD took his legal advisor J.D. Choksi, and Moolgaokar with him. The situation was not very favourable for the Tatas but the Chairman of Daimler-Benz took charge of the meeting and gave JRD the opportunity to draft the agreement, 'You draft the agreement and we'll discuss it.'

But keeping the differences aside in 1954 the agreement between the two companies was at last finalised. The Tatas got the order of making the trucks and a new beginning for the Tatas was initiated. But as we know that nothing comes with absolute easiness, the path of TELCO was filled with bumps and the next bump came in the middle of 1950. It was the time when Prime Minister Jawaharlal Nehru thought that there should be a controlled increase in the production of trucks and locomotives. But this problem was soon resolved after JRD with Moolgaokar met with the industry minister T.T. Krishnamachari. He allowed the Tatas to continue their business with Daimler-Benz without creating any unnecessary problems.

The collaboration between the Tatas and the Benz was quite satisfying as both the companies, and especially JRD, always wanted perfection. The truck production was going smoothly but, the locomotive production was not quite smooth due to the railways' policy. The perfection and skill of the Tata engineers were the prime reason for this happy collaboration. Moolgaokar working for the TELCO always tried to brush up the skills of the workers and also tried to make the company a bit more sophisticated. Moolgaokar's approach to work was not much appreciated by the other members of the Board but JRD always supported him. Eventually, the skills of the engineers were becoming more perfect with time.

This standard of the Tatas helped them to sell trucks at a price of Rs. 40.000/- in the year 1970 and, they never increased the price of the trucks even if the demand was increasing. According to Moolgaokar, 'Profits should come from productivity and not by raising prices in a favourable market' and 'Our greatest asset is customer affection.' It was JRD's vision and understanding that let him give all the responsibilities of TELCO to Moolgaokar because of his excellence. JRD and Sumant Moolgaokar both were men of perfection and utmost sincerity and, that is reason development of both TISCO and TELCO was only increasing.

❑

New Era of IT Sectors

JRD was fast becoming a business tycoon and was opening new companies to expand their industry. Among a lot of remarkable sectors that Tata Sons had opened one was Tata Consultancy Services or TCS. It is now India's second-largest IT company having many branches all over India. Tata Consultancy Services did not start as per the name it is today. The Tatas and especially JRD Tata always leaned towards having skilled workers in the company. This was one of the major reasons that Tata Sons was expanding smoothly and also was in demand. In the year 1962, Tata Sons decided to open a new consultancy service. This new company Tata Electric Company had a tie-up with another company called Ebasco situated in America. Soon this company started to get involved in a broader spectrum of power fields, fertilisers, chemicals, engineering, etc. In 1968 the name of the company was changed to Tata Consulting Engineers.

As we have discussed over and over again about how farsighted JRD was, it is easy to contemplate that JRD could figure out the need for computers in an evolving India. Also, his acquaintance with Dr. Homi Bhabha poured more light on the concept of building computers for research purposes. Dr. Bhabha made the first-ever computer for the Tata Institute of Fundamental Research or TIFR in India. The Tatas were the first-ever company to start a software division understanding the importance of computers in the future. It was the beginning of Tata Consultancy Services. TCS had professional workers to maintain the high standards of the Tatas. It was becoming so popular and efficient with time that it got a big opportunity to get associated with the second largest company in the world —Burroughs Corporation of America. The Tatas collaborated with this amazing company and became Tata Burroughs, and which later turned into Tata Unisys. Even Mahatma Gandhi said, 'Tatas represent the true spirit for adventure. Tata Sports Foundation are trying their best to keep that spirit alive.'

❑

Saga of Disappointment

It seems like JRD Tata had always seen ups during his time in business. Even though from the outside it was looking as if JRD was experiencing the best time in his business, it definitely came with a pinch of salt. The path of the Tatas was for sure bumpy and the Indian government too came out as bumps of that road. There were a lot of times when the government created some difficulties, not intentionally, but it definitely affected the business of Tatas. The post-independence time for JRD and Tata Sons was both beneficial and problematic. On the one hand, they were expanding their business launching consultancy services, but on the other hand, the concept of nationalising companies was creating a lot of difficulties for them. This was the time when JRD was not having much support from the government; rather, the government was not favouring him at all. In the meantime, with the introduction of new policies, the industry was going to be divided into three parts:

- Exclusive departments under the state. Like—railways, air transport, arms and ammunition, etc.
- Companies and sectors that are progressively owned by the state.
- Industries that were left to the private companies to develop.

Everything was changing massively and new policies were coming every now and then. The first shocker for JRD and the Tatas was in the year 1956. This was the year when an ordinance was declared to nationalise all the insurance companies. The Tatas had an insurance company called New India Assurance Company since 1919. Due to this ordinance, this company of the Tatas was nationalised overnight. After a few years, in 1973, another company called General Insurance was again nationalised. It was very devastating for JRD. In 1990, JRD was invited to a luncheon at the nationalised New India Assurance Company where he almost had an outburst. This nationalising and taking over the company at less than the cash value of assets was in a way depreciating the currency which was totally 'a fraud' according to JRD Tata.

The string of getting disheartened continued for JRD as three companies that the Tatas had put so much effort into — the domestic airline, the international airline, and New India were nationalised. The shock came back-to-back within four years and left JRD totallydevastated. It was not only the fear of losing companies but also politicians becoming superior to everyone. He even wrote to Dinshaw Daji,JRD's old solicitor in a letter replying to Gandhiji's comment, (Author please tell which comment by Gandhiji) 'As usual Gandhiji saw things with deep intuition. In the almost universal cry for nationalisation in this country, no one seems to think of the potential danger of concentrating enormous economic power into the hands of a small political-cum-bureaucratic minority.' (*Beyond the Last Blue Mountain,* R.M. Lala)

Even though it seemed that JRD did not like the government, the case was that he thought politicians would not understand all the concepts of business. He approved the idea of the government starting public sector but the lack of efficiency the government had and the future possibility of state capitalism scared JRD very much. The government was also creating difficult situations for JRD by not approving certain applications of Tata's steel plant. Morarji Desai the finance minister was delaying the applications of Tata Steel and also was insisting that the Tatas should charge a premium on the new issue. Due to this, the dividend that was initially 8.25 per cent came down to 6.80 per cent.

JRD even wrote to Morarji Desai saying, 'I hope you will not mind my expressing some surprise that the Government should take such detailed interest and intervene in a matter which involved no important question of policy or principle but only commercial and financial judgement on a simple business issue. Would it be wrong of me to regret the passing of the days when businessmen with a good record of efficiency and integrity could be trusted to make such decisions themselves?' (*Beyond the Last Blue Mountain,* R.M. Lala)

The problems did not end with this. It continued even further causing problems in a sector that was very close to JRD's heart. It was related to Air-India. The Secretary of the Transport and Communications Ministry M.M. Philips created a lot of issues for JRD totally ignoring the fact that JRD Tata was the Chairman of Air-India. JRD was very annoyed (Author check 'pissed off', too colloquial) with some of the irrational decisions that Philips made. Treating the bureaucrats lightly was not something that JRD supported at all. He tried to convey his concern to Mr. Philips through letters but the response he got was not the ideal one. JRD Tata had to go to the extent of writing to Professor Humayun Kabir, the Minister for Civil Aviation.

JRD wrote to Humayun Kabir: 'I, however, stand by my view that Government should recognise the accepted convention under which the Chairman of a Board is extended the courtesy of being consulted before Government make a new appointment to a Board.' And continued on by saying, 'If the Government wants non-officials, such as myself, to undertake the task and responsibility of being the Chairman of a Government Corporation, they must, in fairness, treat them as any head of an organisation expects to be treated. I do not see what Government can lose by sounding a Corporation's Chairman before making an appointment when the final decision is wholly and indisputably theirs.' (*Beyond the Last Blue Mountain,* R.M. Lala)

JRD Tata was one of a kind and that is why he thought different from others. His thought process was diverse and unique and this was one of the reasons he started fighting early for this issue. His fight against the injustice of government did not stop at all and even stretched when Indira Gandhi became the prime minister of India. JRD approached Indira Gandhi to resolve this problem but the solution was not sufficient. Hustling with the government was definitely draining the energy of JRD but he was gaining pleasure from the workshop he built in his house.

❑

Continuing the Lineage as a Philanthropist

Even though JRD seemed very astute and business-oriented, he had another side to his personality—of a philanthropist, something unique for a businessman. But it was kind of present in the blood of the Tata family. Many people often think that the concept of philanthropy was not usual in India. It is believed that the West, mainly the United States, gave birth to this whole new idea of philanthropy. But as we come to know about the Tatas, we see that this concept was definitely present in India too. The concept of philanthropy can be easily misjudged with charity. Philanthropy and charity both have some similar characteristics but they are not completely the same. Charity means helping people in a wide range. For example, it can be helping beggars, donating money to religious institutions or educational institutions, helping in medical emergencies, etc., while philanthropy includes institutionalisation of all these acts and much more.

Philanthropy cannot be separated from ethics because it has the power to affect other people as well. A philanthropist needs to have certain ethics while working for sectors, like— health, nutrition, education, supporting powerless and backward groups of people, etc. India is such a country where unethical philanthropists can harm the environment or the people of India very easily. And that is why the ethics of philanthropy is very important. JRD Tata was totally an ethical philanthropist who followed his great ancestors as well as his own instinct.

The Tatas not only hold a respectable position in the world of business but have also worked as a philanthropic institution for ages. And this great mission was initiated by the great, the one and only Jamsetji Tata. He was very keen on helping people but also kept certain ethics to maintain so that it could set an example for others. It was in the year

1892 when the British government allowed India to apply for Indian Civil Services (ICS). Jamsetji thought of it as a great opportunity for so many Indians and truly wanted people to take up this opportunity. Not only this, he also wanted Indian doctors go to abroad for their studies to become more efficient. This was the time when on the one hand India was not independent, and on the other hand, women were neglected like doormats, and for obvious reasons, women's education did not draw the minimum of attention.

Unlike other people, Jamsetji understood the need for women's education and especially the need for women doctors. It was almost a regular incident where women would feel uncomfortable to visit a male doctor during their pregnancy and die during childbirth. It was a painful scenario for Jamsetji and he decided to send two female doctors to England to study and become specialised in gynaecology. It was indeed a bold and thoughtful step taken by Jamsetji Tata. But being the great thinker, he decided not to offer them money but to lend it: 'I can afford to give but I prefer to lend'.

This process was returning the money was started so that others could also take the benefit of it and utilise it for their higher studies. And within the next hundred years, over two thousand students took the opportunity provided by the J.N. Tata Endowment for the Higher Education and went abroad for further studies. Jamsetji was not the only person believing in the concept of philanthropy. The next generation of Sir Ratan Tata and Sir Dorab Tata was also the same and worked for the country throughout their lives. After their deaths, the legacy was continued by none other than JRD Tata.

JRD too believed in philanthropy like his predecessors and wanted a developed and happy country. He first got involved in this field when he was appointed as a trustee of the Sir Dorabji Tata Trust in the year 1932. But as we know JRD had his own unique vision which he merged with his family traditions. This could be understood better after knowing JRD's concept during the establishment of Tata Memorial Hospital. JRD Tata was an active member while establishing this hospital in 1937. The confusion other trustee members were having was about the numbers of the beds the hospital should have. Most of the trustee members were concerned about controlling the expenses of the hospital. But JRD being JRD, thought about one of the very important aspects of a hospital—research. His vision combined all the necessary aspects of a hospital—treatment, education, and research. He understood very well that research is also necessary to increase the efficiency of future doctors.

JRD's vision came true in 1941 during the inauguration of the Tata Memorial Hospital. During the inaugural ceremony, Sir Roger Lumley, the Governor of Bombay said, 'This hospital will become a spearhead of the attack on cancer in this country, providing not only a centre where specialised treatment can be given but also one from which the knowledge of new methods of treatment and diagnosis will go out to doctors and hospitals throughout the country.' (*Beyond the Last Blue Mountain,* R.M. Lala) This assumption was indeed true and many doctors who got trained from the Tata Memorial Hospital are working efficiently all over the country. Not only a hospital but JRD also encouraged Dr. Homi Bhabha to open a research centre in India.

JRD Tata had a large view of various things. Once, his visit to France and meeting Professor Jean Capelle, Director-General of Education, Paris, initiated the need for an educational institute specialising in mathematics. But his agenda was misinterpreted by both Indira Gandhi the then Prime Minister, and the former Maharaja of Kashmir, Dr. Karan Singh who was the Secretary. JRD's focusing more on mathematics considering it as a helpful subject made him sound like an elitist to Dr. Karan Singh. Indira Gandhi too had a similar feeling as Dr. Singh. That was the prime reason why JRD's dream about making such an institute remained unfulfilled. Even though his plan for this project failed miserably, he did not stop thinking about people and working for them. Later, he made one of the most beautiful theatres called the Tata Theatre. This theatre was the epitome of Indian art and culture and reflected JRD Tata's rich taste in the cultural sector as well.

John Canning in his book *100 Great Modern Lives* has mentioned only two Indians who were selfless and worked for the nation and the people living it, Mahatma Gandhi and Jamsetji Tata. The legacy of Tata's philanthropic activities was mentioned in the book:

'Probably no other family has ever contributed as much in the way of wise guidance, economic development, and advancing philanthropy, to any country as the Tatas have to India, both before and since Independence.' *(100 Great Modern Lives)*

JRD was not only a businessman but he was also very respectful towards women and valued their talent. But in the early days, JRD had certain reservations regarding women. He was always keen on searching for real talent. Once, for the role of 'Development Engineer' JRD's company published an advertisement categorically mentioning ladies not to apply for the role. This was definitely intriguing, and naturally, a young girl got very irritated with this kind of advertisement. The sense of discrimination and feeling of inferiority made that girl write a postcard to the chairman of that automobile company who was none other than JRD Tata. JRD was one of a kind; he called that young girl to his office and to everyone's surprise hired her for the designated role of 'Development Engineer'.

This gesture of JRD totally changed the future for women and opened a new sector of opportunities. After this huge decision by such a big industrialist, many women got jobs in the automobile sector. This historical incident happened with Sudha Murthy, the chairperson of Infosys. Mrs. Sudha Murthy once shared two incidents provinghow humane and humble JRD was. Murthy said that once she was waiting for her husband to to pick her up after work. It was getting late and dark. JRD Tata spotted her standing alone and asked her the reason. When she told him the reason, JRD also stood there with her waiting until Sudha Murthy's husband came. The chairman of a renowned company did not feel even a bit uncomfortable standing with his employee and waiting for her. This shows how humble JRD Tata was and how respectful he was towards his employees. After Murthy's husband arrive JRD even said, 'Young lady, tell your husband never to make his wife wait again.'

Another incident that happened with Sudha Murthy is a vivid example of how supportive JRD was even with his employees. He truly thought about people with his heart and helped them to make the right decisions which were not always in JRD's favour. The year 1982 was full of doubts and stressful too for Sudha Murthy. She had to resign from her job at TELCO. JRD asked Murthy why she was resigning from her job. Sudha Murthy told JRD Tata that her husband was planning to open an IT industry and she needed to support him in setting up a new company. But she was doubtful about this decision. JRD provided a sense of relief to her by saying, "Never start with diffidence. Always start with confidence. When you are successful you must give back to society. Society gives us so much; we must reciprocate. I wish you all the best." These words coming from an experienced and wise man definitely mattered to Sudha Murthy. She supported her husband and established a company, Infosys. This not only proves that JRD Tata was supportive and humane but also shows how farsighted he was.

❑

Influence of the Great Leader

We know that Jehangir Ratanji Dadabhoy Tata was different from others and did not get easily influenced by other people. But there was one person who had a great influence upon JRD— the Father of the Nation Mahatma Gandhi. Mahatma Gandhi had always been in touch with the Tata family since his days in South Africa. He was a dear and respected one to the Tatas. Back in the days in the year 1909, when Mahatma Gandhi was staying in South Africa

Sir Ratan Tata helped him with Rs. 25,000 and also sent a letter to him. This was to help Gandhiji during his protest against the apartheid government of South Africa. This was not the only time Gandhiji received help from Sir Ratan Tata. Over one year during his Satyagraha Movement, Mahatma Gandhi received several funds from Sir Ratan Tata.

Gandhiji's friendship with the Tatas was strong and that is why he also visited Jamshedpur quite a few times. Gandhiji considered Sir Ratan Tata as his dear friend even though Sir Ratan Tata was an industrialist. The bond between JRD and Mahatma Gandhi was initiated because both had similar beliefs about the worldview. Both of them believed in the need for trusteeship and also in helping the less privileged people who mainly belonged to the labour class. Gandhiji, during one of his visits to Jamshedpur gave a speech about his view of capitalists' relation to labour:

'I have always said that my ideal is that capital and labour should supplement and help each other. They should be a great family living in unity and harmony, capital not only looking to the material welfare of the labourers but their moral welfare also—capitalists being trustees for the welfare of the labouring classes under them.' (*JRD Tata and the Ethics of Philanthropy,* Sundar Sarukkai)

Gandhiji's thought process regarding the welfare of the labour class influenced JRD Tata hugely. It seemed like

JRD had come under a spell which he could not ignore for the rest of his life. JRD always acknowledged Gandhiji's influence upon him. Once he wrote in a letter, 'I naturally agree with the sentiments you have expressed in your letters and your references to Bapuji's teachings and ideals, now so neglected. I do my best to live up to them in a true spirit of trusteeship in the conduct of such business as is within my responsibility.' (*JRD Tata and the Ethics of Philanthropy,* Sundar Sarukkai)

JRD despite being a leader for labour welfare in the nation, strongly believed in Gandhiji's principles about the fundamental issues regarding this matter. There are a lot of labour welfare schemes that JRD himself introduced in his companies for the betterment of hardworking people. These schemes were even followed by the government of India later and were called labour laws.

It was not always smooth sailing between JRD and Gandhiji. They also had their differences in certain cases. Gandhi did not approve of the plan to visit England and the United States by some industrialists where JRD was also included. This plan of going to the West before independence was not acceptable to Gandhi at all. On the other hand, JRD being an industrialist too was unpleased with some of the ideas that Gandhi had about the Indian economy. However, this clash of ideas and actions did not affect their relationship.

JRD still had a lot of respect for Mahatma Gandhi and was still under his great influence on the concept of trusteeship. He followed Gandhiji's ideas about trusteeship throughout his whole life and worked according to them. He himself was the trustee of many foundations but never behaved like an owner. His projection of trusteeship was different and liberal. JRD wanted other well-established business enterprises to imbibe this concept of trusteeship as well to improve the state of common people.

It is not only Gandhiji who influenced JRD Tata in the area of trusteeship but it was also his great ancestor Jamsetji Tata who also had similar faiths and values about trusteeship. Jamsetji, who started the concept of philanthropy in the Tata family, also had a great understanding of trusteeship and why it was needed. JRD followed Jamsetji's path from the beginning and eventually became the great man he was. This concept was very valuable to JRD. To state the importance of trusteeship, JRD once stated that even though the Tatas had only a 4 percent share in TISCO, the Tatas were always very dedicated to the development of this company. TISCO is a company that is synonymous with the name of the Tatas. JRD once in an interview said, 'We were merely leading and managing and sponsoring what we felt, in the totality of the various companies, was a large national enterprise.' (*JRD Tata and the Ethics of Philanthropy,* Sundar Sarukkai)

This foundation of beliefs portrays Jamsetji's vision to industrialise India and make it a self-sufficient country. Jamsetji always believed that Indian people could only enjoy independence if they started getting economically stable. This great belief was the reason behind Jamsetji and the next generation of the Tatas trying to work for India in different industries treating it as almost a national duty.

❑

Different Sides of one Coin: Industrialist & Humanistic

JRD Tata was always caught between two situations starting from his early childhood —the cultures of France and India; an adventurous free spirit being an heir of such an important industrial family having a huge burden of responsibilities, JRD struggled a bit to find balance in his life. He had a childhood where he experienced a lot of changes happening all around the world. Be it the two World Wars or the Russian Revolution or India experiencing independence after a long period of torture—all of these incidents impacted JRD. Not only social situations but also political situations caught JRD in a difficult position. On the one hand he had great respect and admiration for the two great strong political leaders—Mahatma Gandhi and Jawaharlal Nehru. On the other hand, JRD did not appreciate their views in the case of the economy. Perhaps it was all these contrasting sectors that were present in JRD's life that he understood finding a balance was very important—to have a great professional life as well as a happy personal life.

JRD's dilemma related to certain topics made the path for him to distinguish between the public and private sector, and how both could be helped simultaneously. JRD was a renowned industrialist but the best part is he always considered helping the nation and people living in it. He had a number of private enterprises but he also worked efficiently for the government as the chairman of Air-India. His vision to expand his family business never took away his desire to work for the betterment of India. He never denied his responsibilities for India and the Indian people. The problem for JRD was to digest the contemporary, distinguish between private and public. That is why while working for the nation he always tried to find similarities and connections between these two ideas. The primary difference between private and public was the idea of autonomy. While private was related to the notion of autonomy, the public was related to accountability. But JRD Tata completely subverted these two ideas and linked autonomy with public and accountability with private. This definitely changed a lot of perspectives about the public and private sectors.

JRD once said, 'I am disinclined to take hard decisions because they would create unpleasantness. But I personally feel, though I may be wrong, that keeping a certain constancy in the way people regard you, in the way you relate to people will result in a good net result over the long term. You know, it is like a family. You can't take strong, hard decisions throughout, fire so and so, get rid of so and so, back up one side of the family rather than another. I know that all my colleagues have their own views and on many views of theirs I don't agree and they don't agree perhaps with mine. But generally, we have always come to feel that we are doing the best that we can and that we are sincere and that we mean to do the right thing.' (*JRD Tata and the Ethics of Philanthropy,* Sundar Sarukkai)

JRD's way of dealing with individual autonomy and group membership shows his sense of responsibility. He not only had a great sense of responsibility but also had other virtues which developed his character and turned him more humane. Even though being an industrialist of such a grand stature, JRD Tata did not lack the balance between being professional, intellectual, and humane at the same time. He believed that physical, emotional, and intellectual balance in an individual is very much needed and it can also affect their approach to their professional life. It is not that JRD had the perfect balance of all these ideas from the very beginning. Initially, JRD was very short-tempered but with time when he started exploring the beliefs of Jamsetji and Gandhiji, he understood how important it is to maintain a balance of emotions both in the workplace and in the house.

JRD Tata respected the concept of empathy as a human trait and himself was empathetic towards other people. But it does not mean that he was above all human faults or was the epitome of perfect human nature. The positive thing about JRD was that he consistently practiced empathy in his personal as well as public life which made him more humane. This empathetic nature of JRD can be well described remembering the facilities for the labourers that JRD started in his company before anyone else could have even thought of. Empathy as a psychological aspect represents JRD's life as a balanced one.

Not only empathy but JRD also maintained moral ethics in private and public sectors which is also another great side of his personality. In the times JRD was living, it was difficult to maintain an ethical balance between private and public areas, but JRD, being of the unique kind, always tried to maintain that balance. One of the biggest examples of JRD having an ethical view was writing letters and also replying to personal emails. No matter who the person was JRD always tried to answer their emails which portrays that he had a great understanding of the humanistic approach towards his personal life and business.

❑

Doctrine of Divine Empathy

J.R.D Tata had always been empathetic to others, while his sister Rodabeh thought that helping others is a cross, 'I like to think that fortune and influence are bestowed upon us as a trust during our lifetime. To be continuously faced with pleas for help is indeed a cross and you carry it with much humanity.' JRD enjoyed helping others, it never seemed to be a headache to him. He never thought that a person who helped others was someone above the ordinary. While his sister Rodabeh took the activity of helping others as something beyond the ordinary, JRD took it as a duty of a human being.

JRD used to listen to people carefully, but sometimes to test someone's dedication towards the goal, he used to puzzle the person sitting in front of him. Sometimes the questions asked by him could be the cause of losing hope, could demoralise the person in need of help. Probably these questions were asked to know the person's intention. A lot of people, organisations, companies are out there who need financial help, if it was possible to count the number of people who are in need, it would be easy enough to show the real scenario. He might feel that testing someone's intention before helping him or her is important because not everyone has a decent reason to get the help, some of them can be with evil intentions. So, going through this Q and A process was important.

A gentleman and a lady came to him asking for help from a child relief organisation. They were working on a project for the welfare of children. Their organisation received a lot of paintings from a hundred artists as a donation and they were up for organising an exhibition. From that exhibition, they could make a corpus of approximately thirty lakh rupees. So, they were in search of a sponsor. JRD asked them 'Everybody wants a corpus. Why do you want a corpus?' (*Beyond the Last Blue Mountain,* R.M. Lala) Instead of waiting for the gentleman's answer, he went on asking, 'How much do you raise per year?' (*Beyond the Last Blue Mountain,* R.M. Lala) He added, 'The corpus interest will be very little for your work. I am impressed with what you raise every year. Continue to do so rather than relax with a corpus.' (*Beyond the Last Blue Mountain,* R.M. Lala) Out of curiosity, he asked a question 'But why are you concentrating more on children, some say it is women who need even more attention? How many children do you reach?' (*Beyond the Last Blue Mountain,* R.M. Lala) He himself knew why it was important to work for children. He knew that children could be exploited easily, they were vulnerable. He presented the scenario of Sao Paulo. 'Sao Paulo has produced 20,000 children who cannot be controlled by anyone, even the police.' (*Beyond the Last Blue Mountain,* R.M. Lala) JRD himself had been in different countries in his early childhood. So, it was easy for him to comment on the child life of Sao Paulo, Brazil. He, as a man of noble intentions, always knew how important it is to save children and guide them properly. The future of the whole nation depends on the children. If the children are not growing up in the way they should, the growth of the nation will stop eventually. If the children are in safe hands, the nation is too.

When the assessment process with the gentleman and the lady brought him satisfaction, he assured them saying

'It should not be a problem. I will twist two or three arms!' (*Beyond the Last Blue Mountain,* R.M. Lala) This statement was evident enough that he was convinced by those two people.

We have to travel back to 1892 to see the starting of the Tata endowments. At that time the British had just opened admission to Indian Civil Services for the Indians. As an Indian Jamsetji Tata concentrated on the empowerment of Indians. He wanted Indians to get benefits from this. JRD Tata had followed the legacy of the "Father of Indian Industry" (Jamsetji Tata). He started his trust in 1944. His shares of Tata Sons and other companies were donated by him to start this trust. This trust was named JRD Tata Trust. Jamsetji Tata established some principles. Those principles were followed by the next generations. The successors were able to keep up the good work. The wealth they donated in philanthropic trusts was used for the people who really needed it. Thus, Jamsetji Tata's principles were followed by his successors.

❑

Man of Integrity and Ethics

JRD Tata is well-known for his integrity, ethics, and social concern. It is needed to maintain high business ethics in the industrial world and to keep an eye on that maintenance process a foundation for business ethics should be established. (Author please simplify opening sentences, too convoluted) The growth of unethical practices is very high. Corruption in industrial life has increased at an alarming rate. Black money, bribes, tax evasion have become common terms. This unethical practice that has started just to make a profit should be stopped immediately. And to stop this, principles for business ethics are needed. Business schools that have introduced business ethics as a compulsory subject are trying hard to wipe out corruption. JRD believed that profit could be made out of any business if there is proper planning. To make a profit one does not have to compromise with ethics, or indulge in corrupt practices. He himself proved that by being a successful businessman. According to him 'Ethical values [...] have too often been ignored or neglected in recent years in the belief that quicker profits and greater accumulation of wealth would be the result [...]. This is a false belief.' *(J.R.D. Tata: Orations on Business Ethics)*.

For the lack of ethics and increasing corruption in industrial life mistrust towards private foundations has risen. There are obvious reasons behind this growth of corruption and unethical practices in the industrial world. Before India got independence, the salary of a government employee was Rs. 4,000/- per month and the value of that rupee used to be 40 to 50 times in comparison with its present value. Back then a small amount of tax was being collected. So, it was easy for everyone to pay this much. In fact, it was said that a British director of the Tatas had to spend Rs.10/- a month to keep a horse as a pet. But after India got independence, the whole scenario changed. The salary of the government employees dropped to Rs. 3,500/- from Rs. 4,000/-. This drop had an immense impact on the private sector as well. Along with this, the tax rate became so high that it was being touted as one of the major obstacles in the growth of the industrial world. Businesses were getting affected as well. These reasons were enough to give birth to dishonesty, fraudsters, duplicity, and deception. All of these reasons were carrying tax evasion, black money, corruption in their womb, and when they reached the peak, these offspring came out and spread all over in the industrial world.

Dr. Albert Schweitzer gave a definition of ethics in a speech in Paris in 1952. He said: 'In a general sense, ethics is the name we give to our concern for good behaviour. We feel an obligation to consider not only our personal well-being but also that of others and of human society as a whole.' (J.R.D. Tata: Orations on Business Ethics).

The lack of ethics in business in the corporate sectors has been one of the biggest challenges to fight with. If the main authority is corrupted, the whole system would be the same. To establish an ethical environment and to maintain that, the head of the foundation needs to be ethical. In the Tata Group of Industries JRD Tata's moral values, ethics were present. That is reason the employees of this foundation were and are able to maintain their high standard. It is one of the biggest achievements of JRD Tata that his positivity, his views towards life, his determination not only gave recognition to him but also to the whole industry of the Tatas. He inspired other employees and workers of the industry. They also followed the codes of ethics. The aura JRD created was so strong that even now the present employees of the Tata Group are treading the path shown by him. His principles are still being followed. Such is his charisma that even in his absence he is being worshipped as an idol.

JRD Tata was the personification of principles, morals, and philosophy in the Tata group of companies. As the leader, he was successful in building public trust. While the public lost their belief in the private sectors, JRD Tata earned that belief for the Tata Group. This can be considered as an extraordinary achievement. In the world of corruption, it is nearly impossible to earn someone's trust, especially when the whole conglomerate is so large. (Author please explain whole foundation) A huge number of people are working as employees in the Tata Group. It is hard to keep a control over them. But JRD did that skilfully. His tactics were brilliant enough to maintain the values in the industry. If the values had not been maintained, it would never have been possible to earn trust. To earn trust, the face which is being projected needs to be trustworthy. For the Tata Group, the face was JRD Tata. So, he needed to be trustworthy first, to be able to keep his promises, to be committed to the company and the workers, and that he was, indeed. Trust towards an organisation can be beneficial while lack of trust can be harmful. Lack of trust can take down a whole industry. It has the power to destroy workflow. It can damage the mind and the strength for taking decisions. Lack of trust can even affect the GDP of a country. GDP lets us know about the economic structure of a country. A decrease in the GDP is seen as a sign that the economy is not great. So, increasing GDP is a positive sign. If the mistrust has a negative effect of 10% approximately on GDP, the GDP line would decrease. Mistrust can lead a society to destruction and once it reaches the verge of it, it becomes too tough to bring it back to the previous condition.

Trust builds commitment. It motivates people, encourages people, and brings out the hidden good qualities. If an organisation is trustworthy, it can convince people easily. If there is trust, there is great teamwork and if there is great teamwork, there is success. The top line, the innovation line, the coast line, the profit line— all of these lines of an organisation have impacts of trust. An organisation cannot achieve trust until it gets a true and authentic leader. It is the duty of the leader to surpass the levels that were set earlier and to set a high benchmark for the organisation. Also, protecting the previously built reputation is one of the biggest responsibilities and in this JRD Tata brought immense success. He not only followed the path shown by Jamsetji, he literally worked on himself for the betterment. He never let the benchmark drop but tried to push a bit higher. According to Franklin Covey: 'Trust is a combination of character and competence.' JRD Tata was focused on his character development along with competence. He never presented himself as a superior being even after all of the contributions that he made. He was able to balance the character and competence part at the same time and this skill of his brought him success. An organisation that has high competence but lacks character development fails in the race. Every organisation needs a leader who looks into the character part and does not take it for granted. The glory that Tata Groups own was inevitable as it had a leader like JRD Tata who himself was committed to the right deeds, right things, right ways.

As a man of integrity JRD Tata never encouraged dishonesty. Parents want to build a safe place for their children. They want to provide their children with every comfort they can possibly have. They try their best to give their children a bright future and this is a common sight in every family around the globe. In order to do that they can go to any extent, even bribe someone. There is the difference between a human and an animal. An animal takes birth, struggles for existence and dies, and it does not mean that they do not love their children. They obviously do. They take care of their children until they can do things on their own, and protect them. But human world does not follow this. They sometimes pick up the wrong way for something good. This decision can have effects on the next generations. Once a lion gets the taste of blood, it gets addicted to that.

Corruption is nothing different from this. Someone who has trodden on that path for once can never turn back. For this reason, we have to protect the abstract concept called 'integrity'. We need to carry this abstract idea from one generation to another generation just like genes get carried by chromosomes. This is like a chain. Here, chromosomes are basically middle-class people. 'Why only middle-class people? Why not others?'— This question can come up in anyone's mind. The answer is easy. It is because the people who are suffering from poverty have no time to maintain a chain called integrity. They are not even aware either of this term or of the concept. (Author, the previous statement regarding poor people is debatable) These people live with the least. They desire for the least. And if we talk about higher class people, they are already privileged enough. So, it is totally up to them whether they will take the way of integrity or not. It is the middle class people who are bound to maintain this. Middle class people have always been ambitious. They have been gifted with intelligence, knowledge and the power of thinking. This superiority than the poor class people and inferiority than the higher-class people makes the middle class bound to maintain the chain of integrity. But with time this chain has started to break down. India is a country where resources are very low compared to the population. There are numerous people who can claim for things but end up getting rejected. Suppose a government job has mentioned some criteria for the applicants. People who are eligible apply for that job. They sit for the exam. In fact, clear the exam. But do not receive any joining letter. It is really hard to accept for a person who has given his or her best, and this situation is giving birth to corruption. These eligible people will try to bribe or pick up any unethical way to get the place they have once desired for. In this situation the authority has a lot of things to do. It is in their hands. If the authority gives up on his or her lust for luxurious life, it becomes easy to maintain the chain of integrity or to pass it to the next generation. JRD Tata had been an institution of integrity of the Tata Groups. JRD led a life of moral values, ethics and honesty. He maintained the whole foundation in that way, and stayed away from corruption.

❑

Prism of Ups and Downs

And this journey of this honest man was not smooth. There were downs as well. He faced a number of unwanted awkward situations and dealt with his quick-witted mind. He faced those difficulties with honesty. JRD did not share a nice bond either with Jawaharlal Nehru or with Indira Gandhi. Both of them tended to neglect the given proposals of JRD Tata, and rejected his given ideas in quite impolite ways. The only time Indira Gandhi treated JRD fairly was during the Emergency in India. JRD Tata was mostly concerned about the economic well-being of the nation and for this reason he wanted to maintain a good relationship with Prime Minister Indira Gandhi. But Indira Gandhi was busy with politics. During the turmoil of Indira Gandhi's political life, JRD sent her a letter saying: 'I may disagree at times with the policies of the Government but it has never affected my personal regard and admiration and my affection for you.' (*Beyond the Last Blue Mountain,* R.M. Lala). In 1971 the Allahabad High Court challenged Indira Gandhi's election and the decision was against her. There was an uncertainty looming whether she would give up her place as Prime Minister or not. In that mean time she appointed N.A Palkhivala who was a Legal Advisor and also a senior Director of Tata Groups. She announced the state of Emergency on 26 June, 1975. As one of the senior Directors of Tata Groups was involved in this situation, it was indeed a thing to worry about. One decision could have so many consequences and it could affect the whole foundation of the Tata Group. A meeting of senior directors was called to discuss this situation. JRD did not say a word in that meeting. Later he talked to N.A. Palkhivala personally and asked him not to return the brief. He did it as he felt that returning the brief was not a right thing to do. N.A. Palkhivala had a huge impact on JRD. Palkhivala had worked for thirty long years with the Tatas and was one of the important persons in the House of Tatas. There were episodes of difference of opinion between JRD and Palkhivala, but somehow Palkhivala invigorated (Author check word invigorated) JRD. All of us tend to see a thing from our own perspective which is very natural. But when we discuss about a certain situation, we get to see various perspectives of other people and such discussions strengthen our thinking power. It was the same in the case of JRD Tata. Palkhivala made him think about the issues faced by the nation. As a way out, JRD believed in Presidential System while N.A. Palkhivala believed that the situation could only get better when the nation was in the right hands. System barely has anything to do with it. A system gets run by people and if these characters are not perfect, it is quite natural that the system will fail.

During this Emergency period, Indira Gandhi showed her affection towards JRD through a letter admiring the perfume that had been sent by JRD as a gift to her. She said: ‘I do not normally use perfume and I am so cut off from the “chic” world.’ Also, she added, ‘It was good to see you. Please do not hesitate to write or to come and see me when you want to convey any views—favourable or critical.’ (*Beyond the Last Blue Mountain,* R.M Lala). Earlier, this same lady treated JRD in a completely different manner when he started a discussion on economic policies. She did not show the minimum interest in his views and kept herself busy with chores that were not so much important like reading mails and doodling. In fact, once Sharokh Sabavala, another senior Director of the House of Tata, told JRD after seeing her gestures that, 'She is not interested. We are boring her.' (*Beyond the Last Blue Mountain,* R.M. Lala). Indira Gandhi heard this and said: 'No, No. I am not bored. I am listening, Jeh.' (*Beyond the Last Blue Mountain,* R.M. Lala)

JRD Tata was a link that used to connect Indira Gandhi and the leaders of France. He used to be a link between India and other countries as well. When it comes to economy and economic policies, Gandhi used to discard the views of JRD Tata but if he was talking about Air-India or the relationship of India with other countries, she paid attention. Whenever a French VIP visited India, JRD received the invitation to join them in Delhi, be it President Giscard d'Estaing, be it Prime Minister Jacques Chirac, be it André Malraux, the Minister of Culture of France.

When the Prime Minister of France Jacques Chirac discovered China and India, two countries with enormous population, duelling over an issue, he was upset. While he was returning from China, he stopped at Delhi and had a conversation with Indira Gandhi regarding the issues these countries were dealing with. Even after talking to her, Jacques Chirac wanted JRD Tata to talk to Indira Gandhi as he believed the two shared a nice relationship and a conversation between JRD and Indira Gandhi would be more effective than the conversation he himself had with her. Such was the image of JRD Tata that a Prime Minister of a different country believed in him and wanted to involve him in the situation that was meant to be dealt with by the Prime Ministers. Jacques Chirac did not even hesitate to share the information he had gathered about the relationship between China and East Africa with JRD Tata. He told JRD about the presence of China in East Africa and the railway that had been built by it for Mozambique. He also shared the reply that he got from the Prime Minister of China Chou En-Lai on why they withdrew from Africa in toto. According to the Prime Minister of China Chou En-Lai, they went to Africa as the former President of China did not want Soviet Russia to become the only one to cultivate the ground for Communism. China went to Africa in order to spread Communism and build up a strong base. But they had to leave Africa mainly for three reasons: first, China became unsuccessful in spreading Communism, and they barely made any impact on African people; second, the points that were made by the Chinese people were not understood by the African leaders and authorities, and last reason was, the things that had been told by the African leaders were not understood by the Chinese people as well. A Prime Minister sharing minute details of a story that he got to know is indeed something. JRD had that impression that this detailed story was shared with him.

When Indira Gandhi lost the election in March 1977, JRD Tata wrote a letter to her saying, 'You have been much in my thoughts these last few days as the drama of the elections unfolded and reached its incredible climax. I can imagine the physical and emotional strain to which you have been subjected and my heart and Thelly's go out to you in your ordeal and distress. However much I have felt at variance with some of the actions and policies of Government during the past twenty months, my personal affection and regard for you and recognition of your immense services to the country never dimmed. I am sure that you will not lose heart and will face this traumatic experience with the same fortitude and indomitable spirit you have so amply demonstrated all these years.' (*Beyond the Last Blue Mountain,* R.M. Lala) The man who wrote this had had bitter experiences with Indira Gandhi. In 1967 a project was introduced by Darbari Seth. It was a fertiliser project and was indeed important for the development of India. It could have given birth to a solar cum nuclear power agro-industrial complex. Initially Indira Gandhi showed her interest towards this project of Tata Chemicals. But later some of her men refused to support this project and the whole project failed. Tata Groups imported fertilisers and that cost them hundreds of millions of dollars and they lost the whole amount. But JRD never let these unpleasant experiences come in between the relationship that he had with Indira Gandhi. He had always been affectionate enough towards her and always treated her well. He took some time out from his busy and tight schedule just to write a letter to her to assure her about his presence in any bad time. This behaviour proves that JRD Tata was a man of culture indeed. He commented on his relationship with Jawaharlal Nehru and his daughter Indira Gandhi, 'We were good friends socially but as with Jawaharlal, I never was able to break through the fence which they both built around themselves. While I regretted the limitation of my friendship with them which deprived me of the chance to communicate freely with them on matters of national interest about which I felt I had something worthwhile to say, such relationship as was accepted by them did permit maintaining, unspoilt, a friendship which persisted till the end… Indira was a very complex person whose character and deeds will fully emerge only when sufficient time has passed after her death for uninhibited reminiscences and biographies to be published about her.'(*Beyond the Last Blue Mountain, R.M.* Lala)

❑

Comeback to the Throne

He handled his failures quite tactfully and never lost hope. That is why the wheel turned again and in the 1980s House of Tatas received an invitation to take up a project, a project of gas-based nitrogenous fertiliser in Uttar Pradesh. Tata Chemicals took up this project. They were said to introduce the Rs. 1,250 crore project in 1994.

At an international round table conference (February 1964) (Author please check year once again) that was held to discuss economic growth and social justice, JRD Tata expressed his thoughts and views on these subjects. He said, 'I sometimes feel that we have so hopelessly confused ourselves with words, slogans and clichés that we have lost sight of simple truths, the simple objectives and the simple means of attaining them… To the extent that socialism or any part of it demonstrably promotes such welfare and brings about economic growth, we should accept it, suitably adapted to our particular needs. Similarly, to the extent that capitalistic enterprise serves the people's welfare as it has done in all the most prosperous countries in the world, it should be accepted and encouraged.' (Beyond the Last Blue Mountain, R.M. Lala)In February 1978 Morarji Desai took a decision of taking away the Chairmanship of Air-India from JRD Tata. He was greatly saddened by this and said, 'I feel like a father whose favourite child has been taken away from him.'

At this time Indira Gandhi sent a letter to console JRD Tata and appreciated the efforts that JRD had put in for the airline.

JRD was used to be a prime member of AEC (Atomic Energy Commission). After Janata Regime became dominant with Morarji Desai's elevation as Prime Minister of India, they removed JRD from this commission. The things that he had achieved were going out of his hands. He endured all these ordeals and stood straight.

In 1980 Indira Gandhi returned to the throne. After she got her place back JRD got back his position in the Board of Air-India.

JRD had a meeting with Indira Gandhi on 28 April of 1980. In that meeting they had a conversation where JRD expressed his distress. He expressed the heartache he survived.

JRD Tata wrote in a memorial volume, 'There are really two very distinct Indira Gandhis to remember. First, of course, the great politician statesman whose total dedication to the task and responsibilities of governing so large a country as ours, so diverse and so plagued by such intractable problems, evoked universal admiration even from those who disagreed with her.

My contacts and relations with Indira Gandhi were rarely in her official capacity. Because I was critical of most of her Government's economic policies which I knew would not be changed, I usually avoided bringing up the subject when we met and sought her help only or invitation only in matters of public interest not directly concerned with the Government's policies. The quickness of her response was sometimes dramatic.

It was the other "non-official" Indira Gandhi I knew well and felt close to, the gracious, cultured and compassionate human being for whom I felt the expression "civilised", in the best sense of the term, was so particularly apt. On the non-political stage, her personality was a many-faceted and fascinating one which responded to the simple human interests and aspects of life, to beauty wherever she found it, to nature, to children, to music or to art. She repeatedly demonstrated to me her amazing capacity for remaining serene and apparently unconcerned by the tremendous pressures thrust upon her as Prime Minister. Busy as she was from morning till night, she found time for acts of kindliness and compassion which added to the pressures on her already overburdened programmes.

The energy of her ever-alert and wide-ranging mind was as boundless as her physical energy, with which she astounded those she dealt with, often to the point of their exhaustion. I was a personal witness to this on the occasion of her visit to the site of the Pokhran explosion in 1974. The members of the Atomic Energy Commission (AEC), including me who accompanied her, were hard put to keeping up with her as she scrambled over rough terrain. I spent most of an exhausting day with her on that occasion, at the end of which she was as fresh and energetic as when she started.

Indira Gandhi may not have been a beautiful woman in the classical sense, but her charming smile, her poise and the intelligence that shone from her eyes were such that the memory I retain of her is indeed the beautiful human being whom one would have wanted to do more to help and will be mourned not only for her total dedication to the country for which she ultimately sacrificed her life but also her human qualities and friendship.' (*Beyond the Last Blue Mountain,* R.M. Lala)JRD Tata was not a man with only bookish knowledge. His etiquette showed how rich a mind he had. No one can question his upbringing after seeing his activities. He maintained a neutral position in his writing in the memorial volume of Indira Gandhi. Neither was he biased nor was he implausible. His comment on Indira Gandhi clarifies that on the political level they had some issues with each other but on the non-political level their relationship was fine. Opprobrium never heaped on her by JRD for these issues.

❑

Achievement along with Aesthetics

When we talk about JRD Tata's achievements we mostly cover his achievements in the industrial field, our main focus goes on his firm and we do describe him as a successful businessman. But achievement should not be only confined to material success. His growth as a person, his character development should be counted as his achievements as well which we tend to neglect. We barely see a public figure's other qualities except the one quality he or she is famous for. Thus, the other qualities get suppressed. There is no doubt that JRD Tata had a fine quality for maintaining the whole Tata empire. But this is not the only thing to talk about. He was fond of literature. He used to read French writers like Charles Baudelaire, Victor Hugo, Alphonso de Lamartine, Alfred de Musset. He was acquainted with the French culture as his mother Suzanne Briere was French, he was born in France and spent a long time of his childhood there. French attitude was predominant in him. His first language was French. He was not into English literature that much. It was John Peterson who brought him into the world of English literature.

JRD used to carry a red leather scrapbook with some golden work on it. He used to write and draw in that scrapbook. The prevalent themes of his writings were love and death. He commented on the themes of writings, 'I do not know why, although I am full of fun there is no doubt that in poetry, for instance, it is the more tragic things and death which appeal to me.' He also quoted a French poem by Charles Baudelaire:

"Let us go anywhere,
I do not care where.
So long as it will be
different from this
awful place we are in now."

(*Beyond the Last Blue Mountain,* R.M. Lala) He was fond of a poem that was written by Alan Seeger:

"I have a rendezvous with Death
At some disputed barricade,
When spring comes back with rustling shade
And apple-blossoms fill the air
I have a rendezvous with Death

When spring brings back blue days and fair…" (*Beyond the Last Blue Mountain,* R.M. Lala)He also liked the poem "Caprice" written by the "India's nightingale" Sarojini Naidu:

"You held a wild flower in your finger tips
Idly you pressed it to indifferent lips
Idly you tore its crimson leaves apart…\
Alas! It was my heart.
You held a wine cup in your finger tips
Lightly you raised it to indifferent lips
Lightly you drank and flung away the bowl…

Alas! It was my soul." (*Beyond the Last Blue Mountain,* R.M. Lala)The impact the poem "Identity' had on him never really faded. While he read it out from his scrapbook, a clear sign of happiness was spotted:

"Somewhere—in desolate wind-swept space—In Twilight-land —in No-man's land—

Two hurrying Shapes met face to face,
And bade each other stand.

"And who are you?" cried one a-gape,Shuddering in the gloaming light.

"I know not," said the second Shape,

"I only died last night!" (*Beyond the Last Blue Mountain,* R.M. Lala)There were some small quotes as well in his scrapbook and he was attracted to those, like—"He took his misfortune like a man—blamed it on his wife." (*Beyond the Last Blue Mountain,* R.M. Lala)Another:

"I was sitting in jail with my back to the wall,

And a red-head woman was the cause of it all." (*Beyond the Last Blue Mountain,* R.M. Lala)"But, O, for the touch of a vanished hand

And the sound of a voice that is still." (*Beyond the Last Blue Mountain,* R.M. Lala)"To be kind to all, to like many and love a few, to be needed and wanted by those we love, is the nearest we can come to happiness." (*Beyond the Last Blue Mountain,* R.M. Lala)A poem of Langston Hughes was found in his scrapbook. The poem was "Dreams":

"Holdfast to dreams
For if dreams die
Life is a broken-winged bird
That cannot fly.

Holdfast to dreams
For when dreams go
Life is a barren field

Frozen with snow." (*Beyond the Last Blue Mountain,* R.M. Lala)He found Henry Shore's "The Nomad" relevant even in the last years of his life:

"When our ancestors found that wheat
Was a good bread to eat
They settled in Jericho.
All of us are settled now,
But in our souls there is a great woe:
We don't know where to go.
I am settled in a fine place
I own a house, I live in a grace,
I have a patio
But late at night when the wind laments
And the garden shivers—my soul is rent:
I don't know where to go.

One day when I say good-bye
To life and wife, and die and fly
Somewhere in a great flow
I shall be free to roam again
I'll try to find but try in vain

Where to go, where to go." (*Beyond the Last Blue Mountain,* R.M. Lala)While he became a full-fledged businessman, he did not give up on his passion. Literature was love to him and he embraced it. His love for literature did not fade. That is why when he was shown the book "The Miracle of the Bells" he could not stop himself from reading out the poem:

"We're of one flame—all kin of stars and sun.
The brothel's beacon—altar's candle—one
The sluggard's lamp—ambition's raging fire.
Saint—sinner—sage and fool—Life's deathless pyre.
The Christ who cried to One in agony—
The thief who cursed him from the neighbouring tree—
All God's—who out of Darkness ordered Light

And gave man's soul the miracle of sight!" (*Beyond the Last Blue Mountain,* R.M. Lala)After reading the poem, he copied it in his scrapbook.

❑

JRD the Jet

He, in his life, came across celebrities like Rabindranath Tagore, Motilal Nehru, Louis Fischer, Henry Kissinger, and many more. Even after being known to such famous people, he remained down to earth. He was not a snob at all. Among these celebrities, he shared a nice bond with Jayaprakash (JP) Narayan, who was a hardcore socialist but used to be quite a genuine person.

'Of all the politicians I have known, Jayaprakash Narayan was, in many ways, the least representative of the breed, but one for whom I developed an unbounded liking and admiration. I first heard about him when, during World War II, he had gone underground in or near Bombay and indulged in the delightful activity of toppling Tata Electric high-voltage transmission towers in order to interrupt the power supply to Bombay…

I personally met Jayaprakash only some years later in connection with some labour problem at Jamshedpur and was impressed by his transparent sincerity and gentle reasonableness, unexpected in an ex-revolutionary activist. It was, in fact, this unreasonable reasonableness, which, I believe, prevented him from being an effective political leader and playing the powerful part he could have played in Indian politics. He was too honest and too prone to see the other side and to accept compromises and would never be a party to the political shenanigans into which Indian politics increasingly sank in spite of Jawaharlal's effort to keep the political arena clean. Jayaprakash died a sad and disillusioned man whose friendship and regard I felt privileged to have earned.'(*Beyond the Last Blue Mountain,* R.M. Lala)

This whole comment on the friendship between Jayaprakash (JP) Narayan and JRD Tata shows his affection towards Jayaprakash. When it came to ideology, they took different paths. But that difference did not appear in their relationship. A letter written to Jayaprakash (JP) Narayan by JRD Tata, "I must… confess that I do not share your understanding of the capitalist system or its place in history. With great respect, I wonder whether you are not making the mistake of viewing the capitalist system as it was many years ago and not as it is today or in the form into which it is clearly developing all over the world. It is true that such evolution is somewhat uneven and that progress has been less in economically backward countries such as ours than in the more advanced democracies of the West, but the trend is clear and unmistakable and I am convinced that those who are today so confidently sealing the fate of the capitalist system on behalf of history are likely to change their mind in due course or to regret the change which they will have brought about. I believe that in most parts of the world the system of free enterprise, far from dying, will be given a renewed lease of life in recognition of its ability and willingness to serve the community well and also from a revulsion against the unpleasant reality—as distinct from the myth—of State socialism." (*Beyond the Last Blue Mountain,* R.M. Lala)

JRD was lucky enough to cross paths with Mohandas Karamchand Gandhi, the Father of the Nation, mostly known as "Bapu." According to JRD, Gandhiji JRD was 'by far the greatest personality and, to this day, the most extraordinary human being I have ever met: he inspired in me, as in most people, a mixture of awe, admiration, and affection combined with some scepticism about his economic philosophy despite which one would follow or support him to the end, come what may. Perhaps the most unexpected and endearing trait I found in him was his almost childlike sense of fun to which he gave vent in a chuckle which he sometimes used deliberately to put one at ease in his presence. He was also, like Jawaharlal Nehru, the most considerate and courteous of men who would never leave a question or a letter, however unimportant, unanswered.' (*Beyond the Last Blue Mountain,* R.M. Lala)He was able to draw the attention of Gandhiji when he had a meeting with him, G.D. Birla, and Sir Purshotamdas Thakurdas. In that meeting, he saw the secretary of Gandhiji, Shri Pyarelal taking notes of the whole conversation that they were having. That incident caught JRD Tata's eye and he expressed his uneasiness to Sarojini Naidu; and this awkward feeling that he had was conveyed to Gandhiji by her. After listening to the whole thing, he did not think twice before writing a letter to JRD. In that letter he said:

'Dear Jehangirji,

I am glad you drew Mrs. Naidu's attention to the fact that Shri Pyarelal was taking notes of our talks yesterday. It is usual with him. I had omitted to tell him that talks such as between yesterday's company were not to be taken down. I have now had them destroyed in my presence.

Please excuse the indiscretion.

Yours sincerely,

M.K. Gandhi.' (*Beyond the Last Blue Mountain,* R.M. Lala)JRD Tata used to be such an important persona that Gandhiji himself wrote a letter to him just to clarify the misunderstanding.

JRD wrote a reply to Gandhiji and said, 'I incidentally mentioned, partly out of curiosity and partly to make conversation, that Shri Pyarelal had throughout our interview been busily writing something. I am terribly sorry that Mrs. Naidu thought that my remark implied some suspicion or disapproval on my part… I beg you to believe that nothing was further from my mind. When she told me that the late Shri Mahadev Desai and now Shri Pyarelal always jotted down whatever you said in the course of your many interviews it struck me as a being quite natural, proper, and useful procedure.

I am therefore distressed to think that my remark, as conveyed to you, may have caused you some concern or hurt and that I was unwittingly responsible for the destruction of the record of the many valuable and thought-provoking things you said to us.

I hope you will forgive me for it, and that after reading this letter you will not think unkindly of me.' (*Beyond the Last Blue Mountain,* R.M. Lala)

If someone asks if it is possible for a person at the peak of success to be this grounded tell them about JRD Tata. While we are losing our senses, being egoistic, refusing to say sorry, this man after achieving so much, wrote a long paragraph as an apology. Sometimes we make mistakes, sometimes we misbehave with others, and sometimes we act rudely and do not even think that our words or behaviour can hurt the person who is before us. We are least apologetic. We are not even bothered about the feelings and emotions of others. No one can be categorised as someone special because of his or her achievements. But it is someone's values that elevate him or her from being normal. Behaviour and thought processes make us different and here JRD Tata became different from others, became special. Maintaining his values till death was one of his biggest achievements.

He had a liking for Vallabhbhai Jhaverbhai Patel, 'While I usually came back from meeting Gandhiji elated and inspired but always a bit sceptical, and from Jawaharlal, fired with emotional zeal but often confused and unconvinced, meetings with Vallabhbhai were a joy from which I returned with renewed confidence in the future of our country. I have often thought that if fate had decreed that he, instead of Jawaharlal, would be the younger of the two, India would have followed a very different path and would be in better economic shape than it is today. Vallabhbhai's stern and somewhat forbidding appearance concealed a warm and considerate personality that endeared him even to the tough British and Indian civil administrators he ruled over after Independence. On top of it, he had an unexpected sense of humour of which I was myself once a victim. On one occasion I will never forget, having requested an appointment with the great man, he asked me to join him on his morning walk to which I was happy to agree until I found that it was to be at 5 a.m. and that he had given the same appointment to three others! As can be imagined, the four of us spent the next hour mainly pushing one another aside in order to get a few words of our own, only to be pushed aside in turn. Vallabhbhai was visibly amused by our antics.' (*Beyond the Last Blue Mountain*, R.M. Lala)Even JRD Tata's name was used as a reference to get a job in the Foreign Service—the Press Attache Section—by Romesh Thapar, a Leftist politician. When he was informed that his name had been used as a reference, he wrote a letter to Romesh Thapar saying: 'My dear Romesh. Many thanks for your letter of the 30th July. I note that you are now a gentleman of leisure, which is quite appropriate for a member of the party. With reference to your application for a post in the Foreign Service, I suppose its fate will now depend on your friend, Krishna Menon. As a fellow Bolshevik, he should support it. I have no objection at all to your having given my name as a reference, although I do think it is a sad commentary on the present condition and frame of mind of the proletariat, that its leaders are reduced to seeking the support of bloodsucking capitalists such as myself! However, I shall cooperate out of enlightened self-interest, as I may one day have to come to you for similar support under somewhat altered circumstances. I would be content with a minor post, say, as Commissar for Industries with a couple of "dachas", three American cars, and a few servants (including a member of the secret police) thrown in... Yours Jeh.' (*Beyond the Last Blue Mountain,* R.M. Lala).

This shows that JRD Tata was a man of prudence and moderation. He was addressed as Jay in the letter by Romesh Thapar. After he read that he had been addressed as Jay instead of Jeh, he added in that letter, 'I have looked up the dictionary, and find that Jay is "a noisy, chattering, European bird of brilliant plumage", and, figuratively, an impertinent chatterer or simpleton. For future reference please note therefore that my name is spelled "Jeh", an abbreviation of "Jehangir" and that any resemblance between me and the bird is purely coincidental.' (*Beyond the Last Blue Mountain,* R.M. Lala)

He was friends with the well-known architect, Le Corbusier.

He was also a good friend of George Woods who used to be an adviser to the World Bank and troubleshooter for its President, Eugene Black. Later Woods guided the House of Tatas, and with his help, they were able to get a loan for the development of Tata Steel.

Woods had a nice impression of the Tatas and the *London Economist* talked about his firm. So, Woods wrote, 'That was an exceedingly interesting piece in the *London Economist* a few weeks ago about your business. I started to say I wish there was more publicity of this sort coming out of India but, of course, this is not possible because there is only one "Tata". You may be justifiably proud of your organisation, the job it does with a minimum of constructive collaboration from the Government bureaucrats, and also of the very high regard in which it is held throughout Western Europe and North America.' (*Beyond the Last Blue Mountain,* R.M. Lala) This can be counted as JRD Tata's achievement as well.

Not only was George Woods his friend, but JRD was also known to Louie Woods, the wife of George Woods. JRD sent a letter to her saying, 'The enclosed five snaps taken by you and me while we were watching the Labour Day Parade may amuse you and George. I think the one of you clinging lovingly to him is rather sweet. If you had been in the Parade there would have been at least one good-looking couple in it!' (*Beyond the Last Blue Mountain,* R.M. Lala)

He went on to say that he had met a lot of people in his journey and from those people the Woods were exceptional, 'amongst the most rewarding experiences of my career.' (*Beyond the Last Blue Mountain,* R.M. Lala)

❑

The Sagacity and the Endurance

A firm needs expert professional advice; the House of Tatas needed that support too for the expansion of their business, and the need was felt by the Chairman, Sir Nowroji Saklatvala. He took the help of outsiders; those who provided the Tatas with legal advice was the firm of Wadia, Ghandy & Company, Solicitors. The financial advice came from F.E. Dinshaw. JRD Tata believed that although these were doing a good job for theTata Group, but he wanted to have such help in-house. He talked to Sir Nowroji Saklatvala regarding this, shared his opinions in a convincing way. As a result of this J.D. Choksi, who used to work with Wadia, Ghandy & Company became a part of the House of Tatas in July 1938. Many shining stars started joining the Tata Group. J.D.C. who was known as 'Jinx' became the alter ego of JRD Tata and rose to the post of Vice-Chairman of Tata Steel and Air-India. J.D.C. as a partner of Tatas made great contributions and one of those was bringing Nani Palkhivala to Tata Group. Nani Palkhivala was the most brilliant and worthiest legal luminary in the House of Tatas.

JRD had fine eye for detecting talents. First, he gave chance to J.D.C. who in his turn proved his worth, and then he took in A.D. Shroff who was in a partnership with the sharebrokers Batlivala & Karani, as a financier. A.D. Shroff was intelligent and had all the qualities JRD was looking for.

JRD felt the urge to start a Statistics Department as back in those days no one really cared about statistics. Y.S. Pandit joined in 1940. Pandit used to work at the Bombay Government Labour Office as Statistical Superintendent. According to Y.S. Pandit, 'JRD had a hunger for statistics. In those days—the 1930s—they were not readily available.

Industrial houses did not bother about statistics. The only source that showed an interest in compiling them was the Government. In Bombay House, we used to compile statistics on different subjects and stencil them on a rather unpresentable page or two. We soon found they were much appreciated not only in India but also abroad.' (*Beyond the Last Blue Mountain,* R.M. Lala)After Y.S. Pandit, Dr. John Matthai was appointed to work for the Department of Economics and Statistics that played a huge role in the development of the industrial world of India.

As said earlier, JRD was brilliant in spotting talent. He gave responsibilities to capable hands and heads. A firm needs manpower, intelligence, brilliant guidance, and maintenance; after being appointed chairman he did almost everything that he once dreamt of.

JRD thought that not only Directors should attend the meetings while the discussion is about the wage problems, policies introduced by Government, he wanted the opinions of the Chief Executives and the Head of the Departments as well. He initiated the Inter-Departmental Conference in the 1950s. The sole purpose of including them in the meeting was to make them feel more involved; and such conferences gave them a wider perspective of the objectives and aims of the House of Tatas. Almost twenty-five Chief Executives used to attend the conferences that were held every month. These discussions made them think not just as workers of the Tata industry, but as a family. This sense of unity and integration is important for the improvement of any company and Tata Group had it thanks to JRD. It is the duty of the leader to lead his people in the right way, to find out the gaps, and to fill them with something that fits. JRD did just that.

He left no stone unturned, he tried his best. He did not succed every time, he fell, but he had the power to stand up again, the will to surviv the fall, and this determination and dedication made him surpass the level of ordinary, made him extra-ordinary and won him the Bharat Ratna in 1992.

He was so dedicated to the development of Tata Group that he never stopped thinking about new ways for the betterment of the firm. He formed a committee named "The Superior Staff Recruiting Committee." The purpose of the committee was to recruit intelligent interviewees. This committee was formed of four people, Sir Homi Mody, Sir Ardeshir Dalal, Dr. John Matthai, and JRD Tata himself. For the very first time they selected three brilliant interviewees—P.D. Kasbekar, E.G. Kakatkar, and Bhavnagri. But all three of them left in two years. After their departure, JRD said, "I never knew why these three were in such a hurry to leave.' (*Beyond the Last Blue Mountain,* R.M. Lala) JRD was able to pinpoint the lacuna, 'While they (the first set of candidates) were not selected with proper preparations and study and that they did not last very long, I still was satisfied that this was the right thing to do and that we must do it again but do it properly.' (*Beyond the Last Blue Mountain,* R.M. Lala) He also realised that his co-workers 'who may have been eminent in every other activity did not know anything about how to recruit people straight from colleges and universities and that we should get professional advice.' (*Beyond the Last Blue Mountain,* R.M. Lala)JRD felt the need for proper management; back in those days there was barely any college that taught management. Therefore they needed to set up their own management school so that in future top executives would be absorbed from there. JRD himself was privileged enough to learn management from someone like John Peterson. But not everyone in this country gets the chance to learn from people like John Peterson. JRD felt the necessity and formed the Tata Administrative Service (TAS). The first person to join Tata Administrative Service (TAS) was Dr. F.A. Mehta. Dr. F.A. Mehta was a learned man. He used to be a student of Economics at the London School of Economics (LSE). After joining the House of Tata, he learnt a lot of things from JRD. As an acknowledgment, he said, 'In business or industry the moment the number two man gets too much attention in the press or public and he gets the glory, the number one tries to pull him down. JRD's greatest credit is he never assumed an adversarial role to anybody coming up in Tatas. He would disagree on policy matters. He would even criticise the personality of someone but he would never assume an adversarial position.' (*Beyond the Last Blue Mountain*, R.M. Lala). Dr. F.A. Mehta once asked JRD out of curiosity if he had ever fired someone from his firm or not and the reply he got from JRD was, 'He had moved people to jobs that better suited them but only on one or two occasions did he have to get rid of people and, that too always in consultation with his colleagues.' (*Beyond the Last Blue Mountain,* R.M. Lala). According to Dr. F.A. Mehta, 'The Tatas are an unstructured organisation capable of doing great things and throwing up outstanding managers, while Levers by contrast are well-structured organisations.' (*Beyond the Last Blue Mountain,* R.M. Lala)The reason behind establishing the Department of Public Relations, and the Department of Economics and Statistics was to increase the comprehension and grasp of the employees.

Achievements and success do not come by themselves. Every one of us has some goals to achieve. Every one of us has our own desires, our own aims. But once we fail, we fear to stand up and defeat that failure. JRD Tata had shown that a person needs to work hard to climb the peak of success. A person needs to overcome every obstacle that is thrown at him or her. Life is all about lessons and we need to keep learning. We need to be open-minded. We need to welcome criticism. We need to be a sport and lastly, we need to keep going.

JRD once sent a letter to a Calcutta educationist saying, 'I thank you for your letter of the 6th August (1965) enquiring what have been the guiding principles which have kindled my path and my career. I do not consider myself to be an "illustrious personality" but only an ordinary businessman and citizen who has tried to make the best of his opportunities to advance the cause of India's industrial and economic development. Any such guiding principles I might unconsciously have had in my life can be summarised as follows:

That nothing worthwhile is ever achieved without deep thought and hard work;

That one must think for oneself and never accept at their face value slogans and catchphrases which, unfortunately, our people are too easily susceptible;

That one must forever strive for excellence, or even perfection, in any task however small, and never be satisfied with the second-best;

That no success or achievement in material terms is worthwhile unless it serves the needs or interests of the country and its people and is achieved by fair and honest means;

That good human relations not only bring great personal rewards but are essential to the success of any enterprise.' (Beyond the Last Blue Mountain, R.M. Lala)

❑

Winter's Tale of Dreams and Departure

This great person took his last breath in Canton Hospital, Geneva. It was 29 November 1963 when he left everyone, peacefully. He was buried at the Pere la Chaise cemetery in Paris as desired. S.A. Sabavala described the ceremony of the last journey thus:'The chapel, entered by climbing a flight of steps, is a many-pillared, stained-glass-windowed rotunda. Inside, on a further incline is an inner chapel lined with dark blue mosaic tiles. Here was brought in a simple walnut, unembellished coffin. On the lid was a single red rose. On a cold grey winter afternoon, the chapel was brilliantly illuminated with flowers. In the dead of winter, flowers, it would seem, constitute the highest tribute and Europe had laid out an unending carpet for the Chairman's last journey. Hundreds of wreaths and sprays and bouquets of the most magnificent coloured flowers I have ever seen dazzled the vision in many splendored rainbow effects. The flowers came from many countries, from many people—big and small—from many organisations. As the ceremony began, at the foot of the coffin was placed a large white dome-shaped wreath by the Indian Minister of External Affairs who represented the Government of India. He was accompanied by our Ambassador in France and officials of the Embassy including ADCs in full uniform. I also noticed several other Indian Ambassadors, some of them personal friends of the Chairman, who had flown in from different European capitals. France sent two ministerial representatives, who also placed a wreath draped in the French national colours.

Then two Zoroastrian priests, who had come from London, began to chant selected passages from the Avasthas

(Zoroastrian prayers) which they afterward explained in detail to an appreciative audience. The chanting was followed by a warm felicitous touch. The Chairman's personal staff had given me a cassette recording of some of his favourite hymns which he used, apparently, to listen to quite often. These were softly sung. Two of these—"Abide With Me" and "The Lord is My Shepherd" —were also the favourite hymns of Gandhiji, often sung at these prayer meetings. It was, as you can imagine, a most moving, poignant moment. As the music finally died away, in pin-drop silence Mr. Ratan Tata led the congregation in single file up the steps to the inner altar to circle the coffin. By its side, lit by candles, were three portraits of the Chairman. People moved slowly, bowed, touched the coffin, bent their heads in silent prayer, and then went back down the steps to their seats again. After Mr. Ratan Tata had briefly expressed his gratitude to the assembled mourners for their presence, six grey-suited pall-bearers came in to lift the coffin out of the chapel and place it in a glass hearse. We followed. The hearse was preceded by another van carrying a huge pyramid of wreaths. Slowly, very slowly, the cortege wended its way along a stone-paved road to the vault of the Tata family, the last resting place of the Chairman's mother and father and two brothers. The grey marble stone slab of the vault was open. Beside it was laid the coffin and here each one of us was able to step forward and shower it with white rose petals. The coffin was then gently lowered into the vault. No one spoke. The silence was absolute. One could only hear the cold wind rustle the dead branches overhead.' (Beyond the Last Blue Mountain, R.M. Lala)

❑